FIVE MINUTES TO MIDNIGHT

FIVE MINUTES TO MIDNIGHT

By

FREDK. A. TATFORD, Litt.D.

VICTORY PRESS

LONDON & EASTBOURNE

© F. A. TATFORD 1970

ISBN 0 85476 087 3

New and revised edition 1971

Reprinted 1973

Printed in Great Britain for
Victory Press (Evangelical Publishers Ltd)
Lottbridge Drove, Eastbourne, Sussex
by
Compton Printing Ltd,
London and Aylesbury

CONTENTS

PREFACE

IT was noon and the church clock started striking the hour. Something had obviously gone wrong with the mechanism, for the clock went on striking 12—13—14—15.... The little girl, returning home from school, listened with astonishment and then burst into her home, shouting, 'Mummy, *it's never been so late before.*' Reference has frequently been made to the picture of the clock on the cover of *The Bulletin of Atomic Scientists.* Until the end of 1967 the hands of the clock stood at twelve minutes to midnight, but in 1968 the minute hand was advanced to seven minutes to the hour as an indication of the increased uncertainty of life in this atomic age. *It has never been so late before.*

In his last great speech in parliament as Prime Minister, Sir Winston Churchill referred to the dangers of the hydrogen bomb and asked, 'Which way can we turn to save our lives and the future of the world? ... It does not matter so much to old people: they are going soon anyway. But I find it poignant to look at youth in all its activity and ardour and, most of all, to watch little children playing their many games, and wonder what would lie before them if God wearied of mankind.' Reporting the speech under the headline, 'Three years to live,' *The Daily Mail* said that by 1958 or 1959 the two halves of the world would live in mutual terror of being wiped out, and added, 'Thus we have only a short time to make our peace with each other or to make our peace with God.'

Over a decade has passed and the world has become

accustomed to living with danger, and fear has waned rather than increased. Yet the uncertainties of life have never been greater. In a speech at the U.N. in May 1969 U Thant gave a warning which has apparently fallen upon deaf ears. 'I can only conclude,' he said, 'from the information that is available to me as Secretary General, that the members of the United Nations have perhaps ten years left in which to subordinate their ancient quarrels and launch a global partnership to curb the arms race, to improve the human environment, to defuse the population explosion, and to supply the required momentum to world development efforts. If such a global partnership is not formed within the next decade, then I very much fear that the problems I have mentioned will have reached such staggering proportions that they will be beyond our capacity to control. . . . While we waste our substance on war and in the increasingly dangerous arms race, we are neglecting threats to our civilisation which should have first priority on our attention.' They were serious words that deserved far more notice than they have received. *It has never been so late before.*

Those who pause to consider the inevitable outcome of the current trends in practically every sphere of life, find themselves driven to the inescapable conclusion that the world is rapidly heading for a crisis unparalleled in human history—and that nothing can now avert it. *It has never been so late before.*

FREDK. A. TATFORD

1

SCIENTIFIC ADVANCE

CENTURIES ago the prophet Daniel declared that a feature of 'the time of the end' would be that knowledge would increase (Dan. 12:4). The words might have been penned specifically about the twentieth century. Certainly the progress made and the developments which have taken place in the last few years—and particularly in this second half of the century—have been amazing, and the potentialities of the near future seem to be greater than ever.

Already men have trodden the surface of the moon and are now reaching out to Mars. They are plumbing the depths and exploring the ocean floor. In a few years' time, we may choose to live on the moon or at the bottom of the sea. We may be travelling on super-motorways on monorail and under the direction of a linear electric motor fastened to the top of our car; or we may be transported by hover-train, in coaches hanging from an overhead track and supported on air film sucked between the track and a vacuum chamber on the top of the coach. We may encircle the earth in a few hours by supersonic jet, or travel to the office from the roof of a local station by helicopter. The possibilities are limitless.

This is true in every sphere. The prophet Isaiah, for example, predicted that one day waters would break out in the waste places and that streams would flow in the desert (Isa. 35:6; 43:19, 20). In the Sahara now, the desert has begun to blossom as the rose, for engineers have discovered reserves of water below the sand in quantities so vast as to be almost immeasurable. 25,000 acres of desert have become a fertile land, and crops of all kinds are being grown where nothing would once grow, and experimental flocks of sheep are grazing in the midst of the sandy waste. Experts confidently anticipate that enough will eventually be produced to feed the whole of Libya.

Again, within five years, a large electricity generating station, powered solely by solar radiation, will be in operation in America, and consideration is being given to placing solar energy collectors in orbit and converting the energy into microwave radiation at a suitable frequency for transmission to earth. Television screens may soon be little more than a layer of electroluminescent material sandwiched between arrays of electrodes and fastened to the wall, and we may shortly have no choice of the programme to be seen and heard.

Our daily newspaper may be produced by a facsimile printer which turns transmitted signals into the printed word by scanning an electron beam across a sheet of light sensitive paper. Or the typeset and press may be replaced by a laser beam and holograms, the material being photographed and a hologram of the image produced by a laser and the conventional optical arrangement.

In the not too distant future, a woman may be able to walk into an official store and select by label a small packet containing a frozen, one-day old embryo (the sex, I.Q., colour of hair and eyes being indicated on the label), and have her new baby placed in a glass womb in a laboratory to be developed for the normal period of gestation. In the foreseeable future, it may also be practicable to manipulate the genetic material to produce bodies to specification as regards intelligence, talent and temperament.

The experiments of Kornberg, Goulian and others have resulted in the synthesising of DNA (deoxyribonucleic acid), the genetic code which is the nucleus of the living cell. The code of the chromosomes, those factors which control heredity, has been broken. Man now understands the codes which give the specific instructions on reproduction, and scientists today are interested in amino acids, proteins, enzymes, etc., in the hope that, in a day not far ahead, it will be possible for man to programme the instructions. When that happens, the creation of life may not be far distant.

Radio-isotopes have been applied to food preservation, grain disinfestation and plant breeding. Radiation can destroy insects or render their eggs infertile. It will probably be used one day to determine how frequently domestic animals should bear young and be employed consequently to control prices as well as rates of increase. It is not impossible that it may be applied similarly to human beings and used as a means of sterilising the mentally defective or the physically infirm.

Artificial insemination of animals has inevitably led to the successful application of the same practice to childless women. Where the donor is not the husband, untold confusion may, of course, ultimately result. At the same time as we are furthering the procreation of children, euthenasia is being freely discussed as a means of reducing the number of old people in the world.

It seems likely that personal privacy will soon be a thing of the past. Apart from the glass buildings of the future, a screen attached to the telephone will show the picture of a caller, while his screen will show a similar picture of the person receiving the call. A laser beam from a machine some distance away, bouncing off a window, will be able to pick up conversations inside a building by the vibrations of voices hitting the window. At Hainan, China already has a ground station which eavesdrops on satellite communication between America and Russia, and at which a £9 million computer has been installed to break codes if cyphers are used.

Turning to another aspect, the stockpile of nuclear weapons in Russia and America is frightening, and now China is beginning to stockpile, and even the little state of Israel is manufacturing hydrogen bombs. Some years ago, Germany succeeded in separating U 235 from U 238 by an ultra-centrifuge process instead of by the expensive gaseous diffusion method previously adopted. The same process was subsequently discovered by Japan and Holland and the full details published now make it practicable for any country to build a small plant and to manufacture H bombs relatively inexpensively. Add to this the dangers of the possible production of the neutron flux bomb—a frightening prospect—and peace never seemed more uncertain than today. One writer points out that in a future war it may be possible by the use of radio waves or by laser beam to disintegrate atoms over a large area, from a great distance, and by effecting their sudden decomposition to engender a disturbance far exceeding in magnitude any magnetic storm. Our Lord's description of the end times as a period characterised by 'men fainting with fear and with foreboding of what is coming on the world' (Luke 21 : 26) is certainly extremely pertinent today.

The achievements of the present day and the potentialities of the immediate future—both for good and for ill—are amazing. The prophet's words have been proved true, that 'knowledge shall increase'.

2

NATURE SPEAKS

THE Biblical references to the latter days, whether it be
in the Old Testament prophecies or the New Testament
Apocalypse, our Lord's Olivet discourse or the apostles'
descriptions, all indicate that nature will be seriously
affected at that time, and that there will be signs in the
sun, moon and stars as well as upon earth. It is surely
not without significance that there have been more
physical disturbances in the last few years than there
were for centuries previously, and many people have
questioned whether these are not an indication in
themselves of the imminence of the end times.

'There shall be signs in the sun, and in the moon, and
in the stars,' said the Master (Luke 21 : 25). The sun is 93
million miles distant from the earth and is a million
times larger than this planet. Its temperature at the surface is 6,000 degrees Centigrade and at the centre over
10 million degrees. Each second, the sun emits a million
tons of matter into space and these charged particles
spread out in all directions. The earth's magnetic field
saves us to a great extent from this cosmic radiation,
since it deflects the particles into the Van Allen radiation belts surrounding the planet. Only a few high-
energy particles normally leak through. When they do,
they seriously affect the ionosphere and the magnetic
field, and the result is a magnetic storm—sometimes of
considerable intensity and violence—which interferes
with telegraphic, telephonic and radio communications
and which has sometimes built up a power overload to

plunge a city into darkness. These storms are most violent when sunspot activity is at its peak.

Sunspots may cover billions of square miles and appear to darken the sun. One seen in April 1947 covered an area of 7,000 million square miles. The resulting solar flare is a brilliant outbreak of an electrical nature, emitting charged particles, together with ultra violet radiation, travelling at a thousand miles a second. Sunspots have been detected from 1610 onwards. Records show that the sun has three definite cycles, at each of which there occurs the appearance of sunspots. The cycles are roughly of 11 years, 80 years and 400 years. These three cycles coincide approximately every 44 centuries. They did so in 1968 and the previous occurrence was significantly about the date of the Noahic deluge. The combination results in a 5 years' period of great solar activity and the emission of tremendous energy.

The first cycle of 11 years has two phases of just over five years each. The first of these is characterised by eruptions of flames up to 40,000 miles high, by sunspots and facula, and by effects upon the earth, but the second phase is a much quieter one.

The second cycle of 80 years normally commences (as far as astronomers can verify) with a period of up to 20 years, during which the features of the early part of the first cycle are seen to a greater degree, and the earth suffers from storms, atmospheric disturbances and earthquakes. It closes with a period of similar length, in which, however, the physical phenomena referred to are not so pronounced.

The third cycle of 400 years has even more serious effects upon earth and this is apparently confirmed by the records of the past and particularly by the traditions relating to antediluvian happenings and conditions. For the next two decades, we are warned that we may anticipate the solar activities to affect plant growth, germ and microbe development (leading to epidemics), upheaval and disturbance in the earth's surface, telegraphy, telephony, radio and television, and even the physical and mental conditions of human beings in certain areas. In other words, what the student of prophecy expects to occur in connection with the Second Advent seems likely to be a feature of the immediate future.

For some reason, when the sun reaches one of these critical cycles, there is also a curious reaction on the part of the moon, which causes what has been termed a 'blockage' of the weather for a period of four or five days. During this period, no change occurs in the weather. If it is fine, it continues so; if it is wet, the rain continues until the end of the brief period. It has been established that there has been an appreciable increase in such temporary 'blockages' from 1966 onwards, and Ferrada, the Chilean astronomer, and Rodewald, the German meteorologist, who confirm that this feature will continue for some time, also say, 'For some years ... we shall hear of more and more violent meteorological phenomena. Some of them, in the field of frost, drought, rainfall, thunderstorms and hail, will be exceptionally violent.' In certain cases, mental and psychological disturbances may be found in individuals. What is happening today resembles very closely what may be expected to occur when Biblical prediction is fulfilled.

There is another interesting feature in the heavens, which may have no relevance to the subject, but which can hardly be ignored. For some time now, four 'pulsars', some 300 to 1,200 billion miles from earth, have been emitting mysterious radio waves. The pulsars may be a form of wreckage from supernovae or exploding stars, but astronomers consider that there is at least a possibility that the 'signals' received may come from an advanced civilisation, which is trying to contact earth. Two giant radio telescopes, a thousand miles apart, are at present being used by the U.S. government in an attempt to discover what is actually happening. There may, of course, be a simple, scientific explanation, or these may represent other signs in the heights above.

Turning from the celestial bodies to our own planet, it is possible to find other confirmation that the signs foretold in the Bible may already be on the horizon.

A century ago the learned Mungo Ponton pointed out that the number of seismological disturbances occurring before the Christian era was very much smaller than the number since the start of this era. This may, of course, be due partly to negligence in not recording earlier events, and partly to the possibility that the Roman world of that day did not suffer as much as other countries who kept no records, but there seems little doubt that over the centuries the number has increased. Ponton says, 'The total number of earthquakes recorded up to the year 1850 is stated by Mr. Mollet in a report to the British Association as 1,831, and of these only 58 happened before the Christian era. A large proportion of the grand total were slight; of destructive earthquakes, such as have overthrown cities and destroyed many lives, the total registered to 1850 is 216, and another 15 happened up to the end of 1865, making in all 231, and of these only 4 occurred before the birth of Christ.'

The number of destructive earthquakes occurring in the first half of the twentieth century was more than twice the number in the whole of the nineteenth century. The number continues to increase. In 1967, for example, there were nine destructive earthquakes (in addition to other earth tremors) and the consequent deaths were 853. The figures for 1968 and 1969 were larger still.

There are a million earth tremors every year, most of them almost imperceptible, but the number of earthquakes which result in death and destruction is becoming serious. The earth's crust is only 6 to 40 miles thick and its centre is only 4,000 miles below the surface. The molten inner core is always under tremendous pressure and its temperature is many thousand degrees. Subterranean tensions and movements have produced faults, and the rift known as the Mid-Atlantic Ridge, which almost surrounds the world, has many such faults, any of which may cause slippages or fractures and consequent earthquakes. Over 400 active volcanoes around the world threaten eruption from time to time and seismologists expect earthquakes to increase in frequency and intensity. The entire State of California is expected to be affected in the not too distant future by the 650-miles-long San Andreas fault. In the earthquake of 1906, some 500 people were killed and 3,000 injured in San Francisco alone. With the city's present population of 2 million, the next 'quake will almost undoubtedly have calamitous effects. In the Alaskan earthquake of 1964, an area of nearly 50,000 square miles was seriously affected and there were 12,000 after-shocks throughout the world. The 1968 earthquake in Iran was followed by after-shocks in Armenia and Turkey. In 1969 earthquakes affected the Middle East from Cairo to Istanbul and rendered 300 homeless even in Ethiopia. It seems fairly clear that, in the western states of America and in Japan, New Zealand and India, large numbers of people will suffer in the next few years, and one writer declares that millions will die and that nothing can be done to save the situation.

It is true that the mirror, already placed on the moon to reflect laser beams from earth, will help in predicting earthquakes from the movements of the North Pole, but this provides no solution to the problem of avoiding the consequences.

It is interesting to note that the Scriptural references to 'the day of the Lord' (the day of judgment which is still to come) frequently indicate that that period will be characterised, *inter alia*, by extensive and destructive earthquakes of the very character anticipated by scientists (e.g. Isa. 2 : 10–12, 17–21; Zech. 14:4, 5). Our Lord Himself predicted that, prior to His return to earth, there would be widespread seismological disturbances (Matt. 24:7; Luke 21 : 11), and the Apocalypse also foretold the shaking involving the displacement of mountains and islands and the occurrence of a great earthquake of a character unprecedented in human history (Rev. 6 : 14–17; 16 : 18–20)—precisely what would occur if serious slippages happened as expected. If today earthquakes are occurring more frequently, and seismologists anticipate an increase in frequency and intensity, and forecast unparalleled catastrophes in the near future, it is not illogical to ask whether these things are not a sign of the times and an indication that the end is near.

3

THE MATERIAL REALM

'COME now, you rich, weep and howl for the miseries that are coming upon you,' wrote James. 'You have laid up treasure for the last days' (Jas. 5:1–3). The apostle John also describes the economic plight resulting from the destruction of Babylon in the day of judgment (Rev. 18). The rise of the future world dictator may be a consequence, *inter alia*, of the economic problems and difficulties of a future day. But the shadow of these problems is already to be seen.

The increasing lack of confidence in paper currencies may well have far-reaching repercussions in many countries. For the last twenty years, if not longer, the American dollar has virtually undergirded much of the western world's trade, but confidence in the dollar has been shaken, and Swiss bankers, in particular, are gradually converting their surplus dollars into gold. (They are entitled to claim gold from the U.S.A. at the official price of 35 dollars an ounce, provided they do not resell it on the commercial market.) The flow of gold from America is beginning seriously to drain the reserves in that country.

In March 1968 the American Congress passed legislation releasing the country's entire stock of gold to back the dollar in foreign exchange, thereby rescinding the law that every dollar note must be backed by 25 cents in gold. Many leading Americans still believe that this spells the beginning of a rapid decline of the U.S.A. in international finance and consequently in political leadership.

On Friday, November 24th, 1967, six days after the British devaluation of sterling, the Paris Central Bank released 10 tons of gold on the open market, presumably with the intention of causing a rush on gold and a further shaking of the security of both the pound and the dollar. Herr Blessing, the President of the Federal Bank of West Germany, immediately contacted Washington and other capitals and held a meeting at Frankfurt on Sunday, November 26th, and the German paper *der Spiegel* said that, without Karl Blessing's help, 'the dollar would have collapsed'.

But the future is not secure, and both devaluation and inflation may be experienced, not only in America, but in Britain and in certain European countries, with the inevitable reaction on public morale. As one writer says, 'Frugal people find themselves robbed of their life's savings and learn that ruthless speculators have become rich overnight. To them there seems no justice in the world and they lose faith in the government and the moral code. History reveals that low ethical standards accompany serious inflation. . . . Here is an instrument that will break down the *status quo* more effectively than anything else. It hurts the great stabilising element in a democracy—the industrious, independent, middle class.'

Such a condition is conducive to the development of the lawless attitude described by the apostle Paul (2 Tim. 3 : 1–4) and by our Lord in His statement that 'wickedness is multiplied' (Matt. 24 : 12) in reference to the last days. The disregard for law and order, which is one of the characteristics of the present day, is surely preparing the way for the conditions of the future, as portrayed in the Bible.

The uncertainties in the economic field have naturally had repercussions in other fields and particularly in that of labour relations. The trade unionism, which grew out of the industrial and economic conditions of the last century, was a necessity produced by circumstances, and there is no doubt that working conditions and efficiency have been improved considerably in consequence of trade union activity. But the wildcat strikes which so frequently paralyse industry and have such a disastrous effect upon productivity, the disinclination to accept the authority of the very union officials appointed by the membership, the parochial views on demarcation, and the complete disregard for agreements and the pledged word, are all indicative of the spirit of lawlessness so prevalent in the world today.

Turning to another aspect of life in America, homes or business may be sacked and burned by a mob for no apparent reason other than the sheer glee of destructiveness. Small shopkeepers are blatantly robbed or brutally beaten up if they refuse to pay gangsters for 'protection'. During the Democratic Convention in July 1968, some men poured large quantities of LSD into the Chicago water supply reservoirs. But for the presence of chlorine in the water, which neutralised the LSD, the effects could have been disastrous. It is impossible to walk down the street in some cities without fear of being attacked, maimed or murdered. A girl was snatched off the street by four men in one city, driven to a park and brutally raped, but no one intervened. Witnesses concluded that the police would arrive too late and that, in any case, the damage was done.

According to nation-wide surveys of the *Wall Street Journal*, 'the wicked tide of race war sentiment is rapidly rising, and unless it is stemmed soon, it will flood the entire country. From its inception in Harlem and Rochester, New York, 4 years ago, the new "rule by riot" movement has been held together and kept going by a small group of hate-filled, communist-inspired negroes on one side, and a highly influential segment of gullible, gutless, guilt-ridden white people on the other.' It has been predicted that civil war will break out in America within the next five years. Reconciliation of coloured and white people seems impossible and a leading sociologist has said, 'The coloured people want only one thing. They think that the white people have been in power so long that it is now the turn of the coloured. They don't want to work together. They want complete power and authority.'

The spirit of lawlessness and of meaningless hatred is illustrated plainly in the student revolution of today. This started in Berkeley, California, in 1964, and then blazed up in Peking in 1966 and in Paris in 1968. The student riots in Paris eventually involved 10 million people in strikes and brought the nation to the verge of anarchy. Four days of wild rioting in West Berlin brought that city to the same point. In various countries, universities have been the objects of attack, property has been destroyed and staff assaulted. The Students for a Democratic Society (S.D.S.) movement is a subversive body, using every opportunity of fomenting discord among students. Leaders such as Red Rudi Dutschke, Red Danny Cohn-Bendit and Rudd are virtual anarchists, and the S.D.S. aim is to throw off all restrictions upon complete freedom, including those on the use of drugs, sexual behaviour, etc. The U.S. National Secretary, Michael Klonsky said on May 30th, 1969, that the primary task of the S.D.S. was to 'build a Marxist–Leninist revolutionary movement'. The characteristics of the last days are here already.

Among other features of the day to come, the Saviour declared that there would be wars, famines and pestilences (Luke 21 : 10, 11), and it has frequently been pointed out that there is a natural and logical connection between these three and that each leads inevitably to the next.

There has probably never been a period in history when war so frequently and so plainly loomed up. In the last 70 years, there have been 128 wars, 52 of which have been between nations, 50 have been local uprisings and 17 have been civil wars. At the present moment, war still continues in the Far East and in Africa and it never seems far away in the Middle East. World peace never seemed more remote than today. A recent report of the Institute for Strategic Studies very pertinently suggests that the reasons for the wars which so constantly plague the world are: '(1) The break-up of colonial empires, whether Ottoman, British, French or Japanese, and the subsequent emergence of new states which are often small, poor and insecure. (2) There are more arms available in the world today than there were ever before in history. Masses of conventional weapons were left in private hands after World War II. Modern nations gave their cast-off weapons to allies. (3) Peacekeeping forces such as the U.N. have proved to be largely ineffective. (4) There has been a rebirth of guerilla warfare, demonstrated successfully by the Boers in 1899, later adopted by others, especially Communist revolutionaries.' It seems clear that 'wars and rumours of wars' will characterise the present age for many years, yet these were to be a feature, according to the Master, of the end time.

In the last quarter of a century, medical and scientific help has reduced the mortality rates in the under-developed countries very considerably. Indeed, throughout the world, people are generally living longer. At the same time, the very high fertility rates in most of the developing countries remain unaltered. At least 24 countries will treble their population by the end of the present century. The 250 million population at the end of the first century A.D. was doubled by A.D. 1600. Today, there are over 3,000 million; by A.D. 2000 the figure will be over 7,000 million, and every eight years will add another 1,000 million.

Two-thirds of the world's population, i.e. more than 2,000 million people, are in the grip of hunger and malnutrition, and 12,000 die every day of starvation. By A.D. 2000 nearly 6,000 million will be living in relative poverty.

Despite the potentialities of the planet, it has proved unable to supply adequate food for the present population and the *New York Times* says that a 'massive famine is inevitable in the mid-1970s in the developing nations of the Far East'. Dr. John Rock says that 'the task . . . is to prevent still another famine around the year 2000. It is too late to stop a famine in this century.' Dr. B. R. Sen of the U.N. Food and Agriculture Organisation writes, 'Famines and civil disorders will take a heavy toll of human life in two-thirds of the inhabited world.'

It is not irrelevant that our Lord said that famines would be one of the signs preceding His coming (Matt. 24:7), and also that the seer predicted famine as one of the judgments of the end time (Rev. 6:5, 6). If current and anticipated events have any significance, the latter days may not be very far distant.

Another alarming feature of the present day is that all the evidence available seems to indicate an increase in epidemics, despite all that is being done by science to preserve health and to attack disease. Vietnamese statistics, for example, show that a plague, which has already lasted over two years, is still spreading.

In 1966 the World Health Organisation issued a warning to the effect that man faces a 'growing menace of explosive outbreaks of human plague', stemming partly from the rapid growth of towns and cities. The *New York Times* points out that, although not infected themselves, the field rodents, with which man comes increasingly into contact as towns spread, are potential transmitters of disease. The cases of plague and resultant death, arising from this source, are apparently doubling every year.

More than 33 million tons of bread, grains and rice are lost annually because of the depredations of rodents, so that they are active contributors to famine as well as disease. It is an established fact that disease and pestilence follow in the steps of famine, and it is not surprising, therefore, that our Lord should refer to them as one of the signs of His coming (Luke 21:11). The increase in plagues today may well be an indication of the imminence of the days of which He spoke.

'In the latter times,' wrote the apostle Paul, 'some shall depart from the faith, giving heed to seducing spirits and doctrines of demons, who speak lies in hypocrisy, having their conscience seared with a hot iron, who forbid to marry and command abstinence from meats' (1 Tim. 4:1–3). Nor are there lacking other Scriptural indications that the latter times will be characterised by a greatly increased activity on the part of evil spirits, culminating in an unprecedented manifestation of Satanic power (c.f. Rev. 9:1–11; 16:14; 20:7–10). Every glimpse given by Divine revelation of the kingdom of darkness shows that the denizens of the air and of the pit are persistently seeking complete sub-

jugation of the human race and its alienation consequently from God. The significance of the apostle's
words lies in the details he gives of the mode of attack
to be anticipated in the 'end times'; viz. deception, lying, prohibition of marriage and commandment to ab-
stain from certain foods, all of which, of course, run
entirely counter to God's will for man.

It is perhaps not surprising that the very features so
plainly described nineteen centuries ago are today coming into evidence and that the accuracy of Biblical prophecy is again being demonstrated. On every side are
people who place their faith in the tenets of spiritualism; thousands of Spiritualist churches have sprung up
on both sides of the Atlantic; literature pours out constantly to propagate the teachings of this other 'religion'; materialisations, automatic writing, clairvoy-
ance, clairaudience and other phenomena provide signs
which the credulous seek. Ouija boards are now to be
found in an incredibly large number of schools and are
already constituting a grave danger.

That, in many instances, the spiritualist does contact
the unseen world there is no doubt, but the price paid
by those who are admitted to such intercourse and who
acquire such knowledge is far heavier than is com-
monly realised. One writer says that, to gain such
power, the individual must 'so bring his body under the
control of his own soul that he can project his soul and
spirit and, while living on this earth, act as if he were a
disembodied spirit'. If this is achieved he will declare
that he can consciously see the minds of others. 'He
can act by his soul-force on external spirits. He can . . .
send his soul to a distance, and there not only read the
thoughts of others, but speak and touch those distant
objects; and not only so, he can exhibit to his distant
friends his spiritual body in the exact likeness of that of

the flesh. Moreover . . . he can, as a unitive force, create out of the surrounding multiplex atmosphere the likeness of any physical object, and he can command physical objects to come into his presence.' Whether all of these claims can be completely substantiated we cannot say, but some of them certainly can. But, as Pember wrote many years ago, to acquire this unlawful knowledge and activity, 'those latent powers are educed, which certainly exist in all men, but are as certainly forbidden by God to be used, or even sought in this life'. The limits laid down by the Creator are transgressed and the individual must suffer for his crime.

The more common course adopted is that of the medium, who willingly submits himself to the control of spirit beings, who are able to draw out his spirit from the body and free him for intelligent communication with themselves and others. There is no doubt that many mediums do, in fact, receive supernatural information which enables them to disclose secrets and to describe remote events and people. But to do so, they place themselves under the control of the spirits and the latter may very well enter and make use of the bodies thus passively submitted to them.

The risk to health, mind and morals is tremendous, as many spiritualists will admit. But there is an even greater risk. To quote Pember again, 'The unlawful confusion brings its own immediate punishment, in addition to the fearful judgment to come. For our body appears to be not only a prison, but also a fortress, and is, not improbably, devised for the very purpose of sheltering us in some degree from the corrupting influence of demons. In its normal condition it effectively repels their more open and violent assaults, but if we once suffer the fence to be broken down, we are no longer able to restore it, and are henceforth exposed to the attacks of malignant enemies.'

The spiritualist maintains that the spirits are discarnate human beings, but the only support which might be found for this is Saul's experience with the witch of Endor, which was one of the contributory factors leading to his death (1 Sam. 28:3–25; 1 Chron. 10:13). On the other hand, there are repeated warnings in Scripture against mediums and spiritualistic practices and the death penalty was formerly attached to this sin (Exod. 22:18, Lev. 19:31, 20:6, 27; Deut. 18:9–12; etc.).

Spiritualists admit that there are spirits who delight to deceive and mislead, to impersonate people and to give erroneous information—the deceit and lying described by the apostle Paul. Spiritualists recognise no personal God: He is only mind and every human being is part of Him. Since man, in their view, has never fallen, there is no need for any atonement. They deny the Trinity, the Virgin Birth, the Resurrection and the Deity of Christ—the denial of the faith foretold by the apostle. They insist upon abstinence from flesh and alcohol and upon absolute chastity—precisely what the inspired writer detailed. Men are deliberately choosing to ignore God's prohibitions and surrendering themselves to the forces of evil, and this increase in spiritualism seems another indication of the nearness of the latter days.

Although it may not be entirely connected with the remainder of this chapter, it may not be completely out of place to refer to what is probably another indication of the end times—the increase of interest in astrology.

In the first chapter of the Bible, God declared that the luminaries set in the sky were not merely to provide light, but were to serve *inter alia*, for signs and appointed times (Gen. 1:14). All of them were numbered and named of Him (Psa. 147:4), and even the constellations were known by name to the ancients (Job. 9:9; 2 Kings 23:5). Confirmation that the stars have a significance was given by the Divine warning to Israel in a subsequent day not to be dismayed at the signs in the heavens (Jer. 10:2).

Tradition alleges that the science of astronomy was first introduced by Seth and that he also arranged the stars in the sun's course for the 12 months of the year into 12 groups, called signs, while Enoch completed the work by arranging the stars within and without that circle in 36 groups or decans. The broad circle of the heavens containing the signs through which the sun passes in its annual course, or ecliptic, has become known as the Zodiac. The basis of Zodiacal signs is found in the cherubic forms of man, lion, ox and eagle, and these represent the four cardinal points, except that the eagle has been made a decan and its place taken by the scorpion. The arrangement is quite arbitrary, and it is obvious that its pictorial message (based on the relevation recorded in Gen. 3:15) has been associated with certain stars merely as a means of transmitting the original story or message to posterity. The starting point is indicated by a sphinx which has the head of a woman and the body of a lion. The story, therefore, commences with Virgo (the Woman) and ends with Leo (the Lion). The order and meaning of the names are the same in all the ancient races of the world. Babylonian, Egyptian, Chinese and Indian records all agree.

Early in human history it was apparently concluded that the signs had an astrological as well as an astronomical significance, and that the future of the race and of the individual could be read in the stars.

The study of astrology has attracted men for centuries. The Great Pyramid, with its four sides facing the four cardinal points of the compass, was probably an astrological building, and it seems likely that the purpose in building the Tower of Babel (Gen. 11) was to preserve a certain astrological knowledge (and not to reach the heavens). The temple of Birs-Nimrud, near the site of the Tower of Babel, is built in seven stages, ornamented with the planetary colours, and is surmounted by a tower bearing the signs of the Zodiac, etc., at its top. It is probable that the intention was to use the tower of Babel in a similar way.

Astrology is a forbidden study, but by some means early man discovered the key to its occult secrets. Ben Adam suggests that by the instrumentality of evil spirits men 'had torn aside the veil hiding the heavenly administrative method and thus laid bare the whole process. Being able by means of this illicitly acquired knowledge to foresee what the future had in store for them, they could have accommodated their activities thereto, and would have been not only independent of the divine control involved in the administration of the times and seasons, but—the future holding no secrets for them—they would also have constituted themselves individually and collectively the masters of their own fate and the arbiters of their own destiny.' Obviously they foresaw the possibility of the knowledge being lost in time and accordingly determined to inscribe the information in a permanent record on the top of the tower which they commenced building at Babel. God effectively intervened and put an end to their impertinence by confounding their language (Gen. 11 : 7).

Fragmentary knowledge of the occult secrets was almost undoubtedly retained by individuals, since traces of it are still evident today. The Greeks (following the Babylonians and Egyptians) associated the stars and planets with practically every known science and connected them with colours, metals, stones, plants, drugs and even parts of the body. They claimed that, given a map of the heavens showing the precise position of the heavenly bodies in relation to one another at the moment of an individual's birth (or, better still, at his conception), it was possible to foretell his future life, its dangers, triumphs and experiences. Each of the 12 signs of the zodiac was assumed to exercise some influence, the sign actually rising at the moment of birth being 'the ascendant'. The influence for good or ill of each star or planet was deemed to be modified by the sign it inhabited at the nativity of the individual. This study of horoscopes was taken over by the Arabs and was later embodied in the cabbalistic lore of Jews and Christians. It particularly flourished in the Middle Ages.

Astrology, and especially the casting of the horoscope, does not belong only to the past, however. The number of books written on the subject is legion, and the study has been taken up today as though it were a reputable science. Multitudes of people resort to astrology in the attempt to probe into the future in so far as it concerns themselves and their loved ones. Magazines and newspapers publish 'deductions' from general horoscopes and regular columns appear in a number of papers. God may have veiled the future, but man is determined to tear away the veil. God pours scorn on the astrologer (Isa. 47:13), but man seeks the solution to his problems from the stargazer. Although it is an occult science forbidden to men, and despite God's refusal at Babel to allow such secrets to fall into human hands, man continues unrestrainedly to probe into the hidden future.

Many of the deductions made from personal horoscopes are, of course, completely inaccurate, but it cannot be ignored that some are remarkably correct descriptions of the individual and accurate forecasts of his future.

This is not a coincidence. Behind the guesses and fictions there is a certain amount of truth. The stars *are* signs, but their meaning is not for us to peer into as individuals, and any attempt to do so (and thereby become masters of our own fate) constitutes a challenge to God. The increased attention given to this pseudo-science today is surely another indication of the rebellion against the Almighty that is to be anticipated as a feature of the latter days.

4

REVOLT AGAINST TRADITION

THE present trend in the arts is causing considerable perturbation to those who pause to realise the implications, and many a student of psychology has asked whether there are not evil forces at work, deliberately undermining the thought life and the character of the human race. Is the way gradually being prepared for the domination of mankind by the Evil One himself? The New Testament certainly does imply that the devil will rule through an evil personality who is yet to appear (2 Thess. 2:3, 4, 8–10; Rev. 13:1–4).

The rapid growth of witchcraft in Britain and America, particularly since the repeal of the Witchcraft Act in 1951, lends colour to the belief that Satan is becoming more active in these closing days of the age. There are said to be at least a thousand covens (a coven has 13 members) in this country alone, and the number is apparently growing. Worshippers of the mother-goddess and of the horned god, performing their ritual in the nude, and paying homage to Satan, witches are unquestionably followers of the Evil One. In *The Witch Cult in Western Europe*, Margaret Murray traces the history of witchcraft to pagan religion, and the flagellation, body-kissing and ritual copulation at the regular *esbats* and *sabbats* give fairly clear evidence of the origin of the cult. Its spread today seems an indication of a determined effort to bring mankind under a devilish influence and can only be regarded as another sign of the last times.

The increase in blatant Satanism is alarming, but is a further revelation of the character of the period in which we are living. Many chapels exist in France, America and other countries, which are dedicated openly and plainly to the worship of Lucifer. Hymns of praise are sung to the prince of darkness, and pledges of undying devotion given to him. The black mass is celebrated, usually with the nude body of a woman on the altar, and in the presence of a grotesque image of a huge goat with staring eyes. K. Goff writes, 'Today in the U.S., Satanism and Illuminism is on the rampage. The black mass is being participated in by over five million Americans.... In many places, young virgins are raped on an altar erected to Satan—wild sex orgies are performed round the statue of the devil—and weird rites held on the mountain-tops in the full of the moon.' A statement issued by the Church of Satan in California Street, San Francisco, in 1969 details its philosophy in the following nine points:

1. Satan represents indulgence, instead of abstinence.
2. Satan represents vital existence, instead of spiritual pipe dreams.
3. Satan represents undefiled wisdom, instead of hypocritical self-deceit.
4. Satan represents kindness to those who deserve it, instead of love wasted on ingrates.
5. Satan represents vengence, instead of turning the other cheek.
6. Satan represents responsibility to the responsible, instead of concern for psychic vampires.
7. Satan represents man as just another animal, sometimes better, more often worse than those that walk on all fours, who, because of his "divine, spiritual and intellectual development", has become the

most vicious animal of all.

8. Satan represents all of the so-called sins, as they all lead to physical, mental or emotional gratification.

9. Satan has been the best friend the church has ever had, as she has kept it in business all these years.

The leader of the same Church of Satan says, 'The only deity that *cares*, is the one that has been banished by one name or another by every religion known; and he has been put into an evil role simply because he is concerned with enjoying life just as you are—or might like to! ... As a Satanist, you will be encouraged to indulge in the so-called seven deadly sins, as they all lead to physical or mental gratification, and were only invented by the Christian Church to ensure guilt on the part of their followers. ... Man must learn to properly indulge himself by whatever means he finds necessary, so long as it hurts no one who neither deserves nor wishes to be hurt. Only by so doing, can we release harmful frustrations, which if unreleased can build up and cause very many real ailments. The Satanic church advocates and teaches *indulgence*.' We have spent so much space on this subject because of its spiritual danger and because it does seem to portend the nearness of the day when the Evil One will be manifested on earth in the Man of Sin (2 Thess. 2:3).

Side by side with the growth of Satanism is the development of another 'religion', equally vile and equally an indication of the nearness of the end of this age. This is the worship of Minerva. Probably the largest church of this cult is in Yucca Street, Los Angeles. The services are attended, as in other temples of Minerva, by crowds of wealthy women and young men, and are all conducted by priestesses. The ritual ends in devotions of a sensual character (cf. 2 Tim.

3 : 6), the priestesses first selecting their own partners from the young male disciples, and then leaving the female members of the congregation to make their choice from those who are left. Evil, practised under the cloak of religion, is spreading and the forces of darkness are making their presence felt as never before. An article in *Playboy* in 1967 said, 'The rules of habit, tradition and authority are eroded. The threats that kept those rules in force—the punishment of God, pregnancy or disinheritance—have been eliminated by the dimming out of religion, the pill and the erosion of family structures.'

In the realm of art, the rejection of the traditional and of the old standards has been complete. There was possibly a measure of justification for some change of attitude, but certainly not for what has occurred in recent days. As one writer remarks, 'When the early impressionists began to revolt against the over-meticulous methods being practised by the later pre-Raphaelites, and argued that a person looking at a tree does not see every leaf upon it, there was a necessary adjustment of balance, and a move in the right direction.' But what has happened in consequence is a glorification of the ugly and unnatural, the violent and extreme. A picture by a modern artist often has no beauty and shows no sign of the use of technique. It is frequently no more than a mass of colour slopped upon a canvas without purpose or meaning, but obviously in an attempt to revolt as violently as possible from the traditional and the beautiful.

Similar conditions are found in the musical realm, where the revolt against the traditional has largely taken the form of the broken rhythm, which had long been used by coloured people in their folk music. The percussive effect of this off-beat raucous cacophony is usually increased by the use of amplifiers and causes a reaction on the part of emotions, nervous system, muscles and glands which is sometimes far from being beneficial to the individual. Recently a so-called psychedelic pop group intensified the effect by the use of visual stimuli, such as flashing lights, as well as sound, and a kind of falling sickness or epilepsy was consequently engendered in the members of the audience. Whether of deliberate intent or not, modern music has become a sustained attempt to create sexual desire and to suggest sexual activity. *Time* magazine says, 'The hypnotic beat works a strange kind of magic. Many dancers become oblivious to all around. They drift away from their partners. Inhibitions flake away, eyes glaze over, until suddenly they are seemingly swimming alone on a sea of sound. . . . The highly sexual implications of big-beat dancing have some psychiatrists worried. Says one, "It's sick sex turned into a spectator sport." ' Another declares that this type of music 'is just as dangerous and perhaps more insidious a weapon in the battle between light and darkness for the minds, bodies and souls of our young people, as are the salacious movies and pornographic literature'.

Censorship of literature is rapidly disappearing in most countries and the result in every case has been a flood of pornographic books, in which every type of sexual subject finds a place—incest, flagellation, perversions of all kinds, lesbianism, homosexuality, etc. Phraseology is used which is not merely vulgar, but nauseating to a clean mind. There seems a complete reaction against the literary standards of a few decades ago, and a determination to shock by the manner of expression, the subject discussed and the terminology used. Many of the books poured out show no signs of literary techniques or 'shape' in composition. Thrown together, with every coarse and revolting detail which a perverted imagination can conceive, their whole intent appears to be the destruction of the old standards and conventions and the old methods.

Films and plays show the same revolutionary tendency and the majority are devoted very largely to the exploitation of sex. In 1968 the Swedish film censor tried unsuccessfully to clamp down on a film which had been sold to exhibitors in 40 countries: the film contained nine scenes of sexual intercourse, including rape and incest. Another film shown in England was concerned almost entirely with the repeated seductions of the 'heroine' who spent most of her time on the screen in the nude. Theatres are packed for a play revolving around what has been described by the press as the multiple orgasms of a Swedish actress or for another degrading play which concludes with a scene of oral copulation on the stage.

Tradition, convention, standards, morality, seem to mean nothing today. Every man does whatever he pleases and what seems right in his own eyes. In July 1969 an Anglican vicar predicted that, in a few years, 'marriage will have entirely disappeared. There will be no idea of two people "belonging" to each other or being loyal. Sex will be no more than a pleasant social pastime enjoyed by any two people at their whim.' In *Marriage Guidance*, James Heming predicts that weddings will soon be rituals of the past, an undesirable institution to most psychologists. At the 1967 Convention of the American Psychological Association it was suggested that healthy adultery would make wedlock more tolerable, that marriage should be for a trial period of five years, and that there should be a premarital apprenticeship period to test compatibility. In 1968 a bill was introduced in the Danish parliament to

permit marriages between two persons of the same sex
and also between brother and sister.

It is little wonder that, to some people, morality
seems to have completely eroded, and that, to others,
the present day seems to be comparable with the period
prior to the Flood, to which our Lord referred as illus-
trative of the conditions preceding the coming judgment (Matt. 24:37–39).

The *Chicago Daily News Service* of July 7th, 1967,
described spouse-swopping as a popular weekend
practice in many middle-class suburbs and estimated
that it was practised by 1,500 couples in Chicago alone.
Since then there have been revelations of the spread of
the practice throughout the U.S.A. and in some parts
of Britain as well.

In London and other large cities, advertisements in
shop windows in certain quarters display the addresses
or telephone numbers of what are euphemistically
called 'call girls', accompanied in some instances by
photographs and details and measurements of the girls
and women who are offering themselves. Certain hotel
porters, taxi drivers and restaurant waiters are also said
to be supplied with cards and telephone numbers and to
receive a small fee for every introduction they effect.
The call girl has her counterpart in the good-looking
young men, who are provided by one organisation
which is patronised largely by society and titled ladies,
who make their selections from albums of photographs.
The vice and sin, which are prevalent today, are almost
incredible. From the strip-tease clubs of Soho to the
'topless' waitresses of San Francisco and the 'bottom-
less' dancers of Los Angeles, there seems to be a pur-
posed incitement to evil, which surely springs from a
supernatural source.

Dr. Eustace Chesser says that one woman in three in

Britain today admits to having indulged in premarital intercourse. One-sixth of the children in this country are conceived out of or prior to wedlock and, not surprisingly in the circumstances, nearly 10 per cent of marriages end in divorce. Traditional standards have gone. In *Eros and Civilisation*, Prof. H. Marcuse postulates the proposition that civilisation will crumble if its energy can be dissipated by free love and an open sexual revolution. Man, he reasons, has only so much energy; by funnelling it into a multitude of sex practices, little will be left to build a productive and prosperous society, thus precipitating a Marxist revolution. Certainly there seems a determined effort, as in Noah's day, to corrupt the race.

Criminal statistics have reached an alarming peak in America. Even in Britain the number of indictable offences is well over half a million a year and it is steadily increasing. Respect for law and order, and differentiation between right and wrong, have disappeared.

Of the awful period of the great tribulation, Rev. 9:21 says that those who did not suffer death still did not 'repent of their murders or their sorceries or their immorality or their thefts'. The word *pharmakeia*, which is translated 'sorceries', is the word from which our term 'pharmacy' (which means the preparation and dispensing of drugs) is derived. It is not an unreasonable inference, therefore, that drug addiction may be expected to be seen as a characteristic of the last times. But it is unquestionably already an outstanding feature of the present day and, among young people, as one writer says, 'Drugs have become the sophisticated way to gain social acceptance.' At the annual convention of the Evangelical Press Association, Prof. A. E. Wilder Smith warned that the taking of LSD (lysergic acid diethylamide) had reached epidemic proportions among American young adults who were bored with life. In Britain there are probably 3,000 drug addicts. Marijuana is the most widely used drug, but it usually leads to others which are more dangerous in their effects. The whole physical system is ultimately affected by consistent drug-taking and it is becoming one of the most serious problems of the present day. It may well be regarded as one of the signs of the imminence of the latter days.

The revolt against tradition and moral standards has not, of course, developed entirely naturally. It is evident that it is, at least in part, the result of a deliberate attempt to corrupt mind and heart. C. Skouser, the Field Director of the American Security Council, compiled the following list of objectives from *The Naked Communist* and filed the document in the U.S. Congressional Record: '(1) Break down cultural standards of morality by promoting pornography and obscenity in books, magazines, motion pictures, radio and T.V. (2) Eliminate all laws governing obscenity by calling them "censorship" and a violation of free speech and free press. (3) Gain control of key positions in radio, T.V. and motion pictures. (4) Discredit the family as an institution. Encourage promiscuity and easy divorce. (5) Emphasise the need to raise children away from the negative influence of parents. Attribute prejudices, mental blocks and retarding of children to the suppressive influence of the parents. (6) Present homosexuality, degeneracy and promiscuity as "normal, natural and healthy". (7) Continue discrediting culture by degrading all forms of artistic expression. Eliminate all good culture from parks and public buildings and substitute shapeless, awkward and meaningless forms. (8) Infiltrate the churches and replace revealed religion with "social" religion. Discredit the Bible and emphasise the need for intellectual maturity which does not need a "religious crutch". (9) Eliminate prayer or any phase of religious expression from schools. (10) Transfer some of the powers of arrest from the police to social agencies. Treat all behavioural problems as psychiatric disorders which no one but psychiatrists can understand or treat. (11) Create the impression that violence and insurrection are legitimate aspects of the country's tradition; that students and special-interest groups should rise up and use force to solve economic, political and social problems. (12) Overthrow all colonial governments before native populations are ready for self-government.' Well might the apostle Paul say that 'evil men and imposters will go on from bad to worse, deceivers and deceived' (2 Tim. 3 : 13).

The present-day revolt is not merely against tradition: it goes far deeper than that. Dr. G. Brock Chisholm, the first head of the World Federation of Mental Health, disclosed the real object of the opposition when he said, 'What basic psychological distortion can be found in every civilisation of which we know anything? The only psychological force capable of producing these perversions is morality—the concept of right and wrong. The re-interpretation and eventual eradication of the concept of right and wrong are the belated objectives of nearly all psychotherapy.' And again, 'The pretence is made that to do away with right and wrong would produce uncivilised people, immorality, lawlessness and social chaos. The fact is that most psychiatrists and psychologists and other respected people have escaped from moral chains and are able to think freely.' This is basic. Get rid of the concept of right and wrong and man may decide for himself what he shall do without fear of the consequences.

This is, of course, the ethic of the 'new morality' of John Robinson, Joseph Fletcher and others. Nothing is wrong of itself. If love directs the action, it must be right, provided it does not hurt someone else. The decision is for the individual to make in the light of the circumstances at the time. The Bible is irrelevant as a guide in determining right and wrong. If the old standards are abolished, the psychologist declares that tensions will be relieved and frustrations will disappear. Sexual licence, in particular, is to be encouraged, whether premarital or extramarital, as a means of relieving tensions. A church pamphlet for teenagers, entitled *Called to Responsible Freedom*, says, 'In the personal, individual sense, what justifies and sanctifies sexuality is not the external marital status of the people before the law, but rather what they feel toward each other in their hearts. Measured in such a way, holding hands can be very wrong indeed, while intimate sexplay can be right and good. You are not bound by detailed rules of behaviour, telling you it is all right to go so far in expressing affection for a member of the opposite sex and all wrong to go farther. No one outside yourself can tell you that. That is a decision you must make for yourself in each concrete situation. We know further that there is sexual contact between unmarried couples that is motivated by love and which is pure and on occasion beautiful.' It is little wonder, in the light of such teaching, that a survey by Vance Packard should reveal that 75 per cent of English and 58 per cent of American male students have experienced sexual intercourse, and that 63 per cent of English and 43 per cent of American female students have had similar experiences.

'A new, more permissive society is taking shape,' says *Newsweek*. 'Its outlines are etched most prominently in the arts—in the increasing nudity and frankness of today's films, in the candid lyrics of pop songs ... in erotic art and television talk shows, in freer fashions and franker advertising. And, behind this expanding permissiveness in the arts, stands a society in transition, a society that has lost its consensus on such crucial issues as premarital sex, marriage and sex education.'

Peter's description of the false prophets who were to arise was never more pertinent—'those who indulge in the lust of defiling passion and despise authority.... They have eyes full of adultery, insatiable for sin. They entice unsteady souls. ... Forsaking the right way they have gone astray' (2 Pet. 2:10–15). Those who have proclaimed the 'new morality' from pulpit and platform will one day be called to account at the bar of God.

It has been suggested in some quarters that the whole concept of permissiveness and its revolt against tradition stems from the radical theology of the present century. How far this can be substantiated is not clear, but it is at least plain that radical theology is virtually a frontal attack upon Christian traditions. This doctrine may be traced to an origin in the teachings of Friedrich Nietzsche. In the last century, Nietzsche identified God as the projection of men's ideals and declared that God was dead and that man was consequently liberated. In *The Philosophy of Nietzsche*, he wrote, 'God is dead: of his pity for man has God died.' The 'death of God' theology of the twentieth century really originated with Nietzsche, despite the fact that this is usually denied. In *Radical Theology and the Death of God*, T. J. Altizer and W. Hamilton take the view that once there was a God who rightly was worshipped but that there was no such God now. In *The Secular Meaning of the*

Gospel, Paul van Buren says that 'modern men are quite able to live without the God hypothesis. We do not need God to meet our needs or solve our problems, for we have modern science to solve our problems for us.' (J. C. Cooper in *The Roots of the Radical Theology*.)

The apostle Paul declared that, 'in the latter times, some will depart from the faith, giving heed to deceitful spirits and teachings of demons' (1 Tim. 4 : 1), and the increase in the number of false teachers today may well be regarded as an indication of the nearness of the last days.

5

THE ECCLESIASTICAL SIGN

IT has been said that Christianity is beset on every side 'by the powerful forces of materialism, secularism and humanism, led by a rapidly spreading atheistic, international Communism', and aided by the strength of a resurgent paganism born out of African and Asian nationalism. Communism has spoiled the Eastern Orthodox Churches of half of their former adherents, and other influences have robbed Anglican and Continental Churches of their members and spiritual vitality. These circumstances might well have driven the churches back to the Word of God and to the Christ of God, with a desire for a fresh outpouring of the Holy Spirit's power; but the principal effect seems instead to have been a reinforcing of the efforts being made to secure a closer union at the human level rather than at the divine and on an organisational rather than a spiritual basis.

One of the most significant petitions in our Lord's high-priestly prayer just prior to the Cross was that a unity might exist between His people and between them and God (John 17:11, 21-23). That a oneness should be established between man and his Creator, or that man should share a common life with God, is a concept difficult to grasp; obviously it could be effected only by God Himself. That there should be a similar oneness between fellow-Christians seems an evident consequence of their spiritual birth into the same family and is not so difficult to understand. The existence of a spiritual bond is generally acknowledged, even if its realisation in practice is not always apparent. Not long after our Lord had breathed His petition, the apostle Paul had to warn the Corinthians of the schismatic tendencies already in evidence among them (1 Cor. 1:10–13) and to beseech the Ephesians 'to keep the unity of the Spirit in the bond of peace' because 'there is one body' (Eph. 4:3, 4). Both our Lord and the apostle were, of course, referring to a spiritual oneness and not to an organisational union, however desirable the latter might seem to be. Since the words were uttered 19 centuries ago, sectarianism has destroyed any semblance of external unity in the visible church, but nothing can destroy the invisible bond created by the Holy Spirit.

During the apostolic and sub-apostolic period, although local churches were at first completely independent of one another, there was a broad uniformity of outlook and practice. Initially, each church was governed by its own elders and deacons, but by the middle of the second century the majority of the churches recognised a presiding elder or bishop as the leader of the local church, although still retaining the elders and deacons. By the end of the same century, there had developed an association of churches, in which there was still a considerable measure of uniformity of organisation and belief. The largest and wealthiest of these was the church of Rome, the prestige of which was naturally enhanced by its location at the capital of the Empire.

The power and importance of the bishops increased with time, but the bishops in the capital cities of the Roman provinces gradually became recognised (largely because of the location of their churches) as more important than their fellows and were ultimately acknowledged as metropolitans with authority over a number of bishops and their churches. Among the metropolitans, the bishops of Alexandria, Antioch, Constantinople, Jerusalem and Rome eventually acquired the higher dignity of patriarchs. Among these five, those of Constantinople and Rome sought supremacy and by the fifth century the latter was generally recognised in the west as supreme, although the former (recognised as supreme in the east) refused to acknowledge the priority of Rome.

During the next three centuries the Bishops (or Popes) of Rome also developed into civil (as well as ecclesiastical) rulers, holding extensive territorial possessions, receiving revenues, maintaining their own armed forces, dispensing justice, etc., and claiming authority over other temporal sovereigns.

The struggle for supremacy between Rome and Constantinople continued for almost another two centuries, but there was a final rupture in A.D. 1054 and the Eastern Orthodox Church severed all connection with the Western Church headed by Rome. The two patriarchs issued a ban of excommunication upon each other, which remained operative for over nine centuries, only being lifted in 1966 (the door consequently is now open for a complete *rapprochement*). Western unity did not continue for long and, in the early sixteenth century, the Reformation led to a serious and far-reaching breach, which has never yet been repaired—although it now seems clear that this may occur in the fairly near future.

Throughout the centuries other churches have been formed from time to time, and the nineteenth century saw a remarkable growth in the number of Free Churches. There are now so many sects and denominations that any structural union of the churches may, at first sight, seem impossible of achievement. Nevertheless, the last half century has been characterised by the number of serious attempts which have been made to repair the breach, and one of the most significant trends of the twentieth century has been the ecumenical movement.

The ecumenism of the present day owes its origin, at least in part, to the World Congress on Missionary Co-operation, which was held in Edinburgh in 1910 under the leadership of Dr. John R. Mott. With the stated object of evangelising the world within a generation, the conference discussed the possibilities of co-operation on the mission field by all missionary societies, the avoidance of duplication of effort, the provision of channels of communication with governments, and other aspects of missionary work. Out of this was born the International Missionary Council which, it was hoped, would be able to provide solutions to universal missionary problems and facilitate the evangelisation of the heathen world. Until its absorption by the World Council of Churches, the I.M.C. made a not unimportant contribution in the field of foreign missions.

Other conferences also played their part. At Stockholm in 1925 the Universal Christian Council on Life and Work, sponsored mainly by liberal ecclesiastical leaders, adopted the view that union of the churches should be based on joint participation in Christian activity and outreach. At Lausanne in 1927 the World Conference on Faith and Order, while approving the aim of union, considered that it was practicable only on the basis of common ground of belief. Joint conferences were held over the next two decades and the eventual result was the formation of the World Council of Churches at Amsterdam in 1948. According to the definition adopted in New Delhi in 1961, the W.C.C. 'is a fellowship of churches which confess the Lord Jesus as God and Saviour, according to the Scriptures, and therefore seek to fulfil their common calling to the glory of the one God, Father, Son and Holy Spirit'.

The W.C.C. Assembly, composed of delegates appointed by the churches, meets every seven years, but in practice the organisation is run by a central committee of roughly one hundred members, which meets annually, and an executive committee of 15, which meets every six months and is mainly responsible for implementing policy. The secretariat at Geneva, however, probably has more actual power than any of these bodies. The primary object of the W.C.C. is the reunion of Christendom and Dr. Douglas Horton, the Chairman of the American Committee for the World Council, said at Amsterdam in 1948, 'An effective welding of the Christian Churches of the world into a single unit, characterised by Catholic continuity and Protestant freedom in Christ, is the burden of our hopes.' It is significant that, prior to the Assembly at Amsterdam, the Pope had asked for prayer that 'those who have torn away from this unity, though still labelling themselves with the name of Christ, may come to realise where the centre of this unity has been set by the divine Master, and will feel the supreme desire to be recomposed in the ranks under the sole pastor'. In the light of this, Dr. D. G. Barnhouse may possibly be forgiven for saying that the W.C.C. 'will be remembered as the beginning of that Babylonian thing which is pictured, not as the Bride, but as the Great Whore, in the Book of Revelation'.

The constituents of the World Council of Churches are of the utmost variety. As Dr. J. De Forest Murch says in *The Coming World Church*, it 'is composed of a wide assortment of churches which have great differences in theological doctrine, church organisation and worship. They represent many nationalities, political viewpoints and sociological backgrounds. They are unitarians and trinitarians. They are liberals, evangelicals, neo-orthodox, Arminians, Calvinists, Lutherans, Catholics and Eastern Orthodox. There are churches which believe in the apostolic succession of the priesthood, the veneration of the Virgin Mary and variously assorted saints, besides those of the purely Protestant tradition. There are congregational, presbyterian, episcopal and catholic systems of church government. There are national churches believing in the union of Church and State, and free churches which oppose that doctrine. There are dozens of different rites and liturgies of communion and worship. There are Soviet Russian Communists, other Communists, Socialists, Democrats and Republicans.' He not unnaturally concludes that 'The manifestation of spiritual unity among such wide diversity has its encouraging aspects, but there are also the seeds of controversy, division and devitalising compromise. If there is to be effective, practical, visible, organic unity such as that which characterised the N.T. church, there is little evidence of commitment to its essential elements in this mixture of beliefs.'

At the third Assembly of the W.C.C. at New Delhi in 1961, at which some 200 denominational groups from 60 countries were represented, one of the most significant decisions was the approval of the admission of Eastern Orthodox Churches with a membership of 150 million people—a not inconsiderable proportion of the W.C.C.'s total constituency (including these churches) of 350 million. Six years before this, *The Times* said on December 21st, 1955, that 'the Russian Orthodox Church co-operates fully with the Communist State and is perforce an instrument of its policies'. G. C. Karpov, who was Chairman of the Council on Affairs of the Russian Orthodox Church, was a major general of the secret police, and the Patriarch and the bishops are compelled to follow the Kremlin's line. Communism has secured a strong position in the W.C.C. and the representation of these churches on the Central Committee and other bodies is so large that they often determine the final decision on questions of policy.

Another important decision at New Delhi resulted in the demise of the International Missionary Council and the transfer of its functions to the W.C.C.'s Commission and Division on World Missions and Evangelism. In consequence of this and of the opposition of the Russian Orthodox Churches to all missionary activity, the I.M.C.'s vision of world evangelisation has given place to the concept of the formation of national churches with a greater occupation with social and cultural needs than with the preaching of the gospel. National churches have already been created in South India, Japan, Ceylon and Madagascar, and similar organisations are being sought in other areas.

The ultimate object of the W.C.C. is to create a One World Church, including the Roman Catholic Church. Dr. John Boutlie, a former president of the W.C.C., has said, for example, 'The ultimate goal of the World Council and the Ecumenical Movement is that there might be only one Christian Church.' As long ago as 1962, Dr, Michael Ramsey, the Archbishop of Canterbury, said, 'I can look forward to there being one church throughout the world. At least, one church with a common elementary structure, a common faith and common sacraments.' 'We Anglicans,' he said, 'hope and earnestly pray for unity with the Holy Orthodox Church.' Yet the Vatican has made it perfectly clear that there can be no question of Rome joining a church confederation in which ecclesiastical authority would be shared: any hope of reunion must be on the basis of the other churches returning to the Roman fold.

When Pope John XXIII decided that an Ecumenical Council should be held at Rome to study the subject of Christian Unity, it was intended, according to the press statement issued at the time, 'to be an invitation to the separated communities to search for the unity for which so many souls in all the ends of the earth are yearning'. Although the Ecumenical Council was a general council of the R.C. Churches, the Pope invited Anglican and other major churches to send observers and, in his encyclical letter of June 29th, 1959, said, 'We direct a plea to all of you who are separated from the Apostolic See. May this wondrous manifestation of unity by which the Catholic Church shines forth for all to see, and may her prayers from the heart, by which she begs this unity from God for all of you, move you in a deep and salutary way. . . . When we call you tenderly to the unity of the true Church, we are not inviting you to a strange home, but to your very own, the common home of our Father.' Again, he pleaded, 'Permit us, in a spirit of earnest affection, to call you our brothers and our children. Allow us to cherish the hope of your return, to which we still cling in fatherly spirit. Reflect that our affectionate appeal to you, to return to the unity of the Church, is not a call to some strange and foreign dwelling, but to come back to your Father's house . . . return to union with the Apostolic See, with which your countries too were linked for their good during so many centuries.' This implies a reunion in which all the concessions are to be made by one side. As Prof. K. E. Skydesgaard pertinently points out, 'The Pope sees only one possibility for the unity of Christians and that is the visible unity of the non-R.C. Christians with the Apostolic See.'

When, on October 11th, 1962, most of the 2,816 dignitaries of the R.C. Church gathered for the Council at St. Peter's in Rome, the Pope spoke of the challenge of Christian unity and said that the Catholic Church 'considers it her duty to work actively so that there may be fulfilled the great mystery of that unity which Jesus Christ invoked with fervent prayer from His heavenly Father on the eve of His sacrifice'. He set up a special Secretariat for the Fostering of the Unity of Christians under a German Jesuit, Cardinal Augustine Bea, for the specific purpose of mediating between the R.C. Church and Protestant leaders and to 'help them find their way towards unity with the Roman Catholic Church'. Cardinal Bea stated that the Council would prepare the way for unity 'by removing incomprehension and erroneous interpretation of Catholic doctrine, by adapting ecclesiastical law to the present-day mentality and to the needs of our separated brethren. . . . A considerable amount of the subsequent discussions was, of course, directed to these ends. As Prof. Skydesgaard has pointed out, the statements made left no doubt concerning what Pope John meant by unity : it was a unity of doctrine, government and culture.

One cannot ignore the significance of the visit paid to Rome by the Archbishop of Canterbury in March 1966 and the statements made at the time and subsequently. The Pope, for example, referred to the head of the Anglican Church as building a bridge and added that Dr. Ramsey's footsteps echoed in no strange dwelling, but in the Father's home. The Archbishop later reiterated his prayerful desire for reunion with the Roman Church.

Ecumenical discussions with a view to union are in progress in many circles. Two centuries ago, John Wesley started a movement which eventually resulted in separation from the Anglican Church and the formation of a new denomination. The history and decisions of the past are now being reversed, however, and a report by representatives of both the Anglican and the Methodist Churches, issued in 1963, recommended the complete unification of the two Churches. Despite the Anglican vote in 1969, the Archbishop and his followers are still seeking means of implementing the report and healing the breach of the eighteenth century. Following discussions between the Presbyterian and the Congregational Churches, a report was issued in March 1967 entitled *A Proposed Basis of Union*, and recommending union of the Congregational Church in England and Wales and the Presbyterian Church of England. The barriers of the years are being overthrown.

Nor is this trend towards union restricted to Christian churches. When Pope John announced the calling of the Vatican Council, the Bishop of Larantuka in Indonesia and Cardinal Tien, the exiled Archbishop of Peking, pressed for a special secretariat to be set up to make contacts with representatives of the major non-Christian religions and to explore the possibility of a closer link with them. As a result, dialogues are now being conducted between Rome and representatives of non-Christian faiths, and it seems possible that links of some kind may be forged between other religions and the R.C. Church. (Many have seen a foreshadowing of this in the title of 'mother of harlots', or other idolatrous systems, in Revelation 17:5.)

Union is in the air and many are asking whether this is of God or whether, in view of the evident dangers, the present trends should be condemned. Was the Reformation a tremendous mistake or has it served its day? It is not irrelevant that, 19 centuries ago, the Bible

foretold the coming into being of a One World Church,
located at a seven-hilled city and reigning over the
kings of the earth (Rev. 17). Whereas the true church is
portrayed as a spotlessly perfect and virginal bride (2
Cor. 11 : 2; Eph. 5 : 27; Rev. 21 : 2), this future church is
described as a great prostitute and the mother of pros-
titutes and idolatrous systems (Rev. 17 : 1, 5), a foul
counterfeit of the true. The Apocalyptic picture is of an
apostate church, unfaithful to Christ, and intriguing
with the kings of the earth, guilty of the murder or
martyrdom of God's people, and claiming supreme
temporal sovereignty. In many respects the details
given are singularly appropriate to Rome, but it is clear
that the description is of a church greater in extent and
in authority than the R.C. church of today. It is interesting also to note that she is referred to under the
title of Babylon the Great as well as the adulteress.

Early in the world's history, a mighty hunter named
Nimrod arose, who determined to found a world empire, and Genesis 10 : 10 states that 'the beginning of his
kingdom was Babel'. Nimrod, the son of Cush, has been
identified by archaeologists with Bacchus, Tammuz and
Adonis, and his wife, the beautiful Semiramis, was probably identical with the nature goddess Rhea or Cybele,
and also with Aphrodite of Greece and Venus of Rome.
The fame of her beauty still lives in ancient history.

Nimrod was the first leader of human apostasy from
God. All pagan mythologies and systems of idolatry
show an underlying unity of character, which indicates
their common origin and all may, in fact, be traced
back to Babylon and its first ruler. Initially, he was regarded as a great benefactor principally because of his
exploits in the destruction of the wild beasts which
threatened the world's relatively small population of
his day. As a city-builder also, he provided protection

from the savage animals of the field and forest, and men were glad to take advantage of the shelter thus afforded. Tradition declares that, in addition, he proceeded to emancipate men from the fear of God and the old patriarchal faith. The Noahic flood left the people with a dread of the Almighty and His judgments, but the Nimrodic apostasy delivered them from this fear and gained for their leader the title of 'Deliverer'.

The great rebel was cut off suddenly, being torn to pieces by a wild boar. Persian records reveal that, after his death, Nimrod was deified by his followers. The ancient world was well acquainted with the Edenic promise (Gen. 3 : 15) and rightly concluded that the bruising of the heel of the woman's seed implied the death of the Deliverer. In brazen blasphemy Semiramis proclaimed that her husband was the promised seed, whose death had really been a voluntary sacrifice for the benefit of his partisans. This so fully accorded with the latter's inclinations that it was gladly accepted and worship was paid to the deified leader.

The worship of Nimrod, under various names, was for long practised only in secret and herein originated the ancient 'mysteries'. Egypt, Greece and Phoenicia all derived their religious systems and secret rites from the Babylonians. As A. Hyslop declares in *The Two Babylons*, the object of the mysteries was 'to bind all mankind in blind and absolute submission to a hierarchy dependent on the sovereigns of Babylon'. All knowledge was monopolised by the priesthood and the king was the chief priest, or Pontifex Maximus. The Chaldeans believed in the transmigration of souls and it was later accepted that Nimrod had reappeared as a posthumous son, supernaturally born by his widow, and it was not long before the worship of Nimrod had been replaced by the worship of the mother and the child. The cult of the queen of heaven and her babe, to quote Dr. Ironside, 'became the mystery-religion of Phoenicia, and by the Phoenicians was carried to the ends of the earth. Ashtaroth and Tammuz became Isis and Horus in Egypt, Aphrodite and Eros in Greece, Venus and Cupid in Italy'. When the gospel came to Egypt, the Babylonian goddess and her child were simply converted into the Virgin Mary and her Son. Idolatry thus originated with Babylon, and throughout Scripture the city stands as the symbol of false worship and idolatry.

Jeremiah 51 foretold the destruction of the city of Babylon and declared that it should never rise again. Yet, when the Revelation is opened, Babylon re-appears upon the scene. The Old Testament prophecies leave no future for the city, but the Apocalypse paints an idolatrous system of the same character as Babylon. A comparison of the last six chapters of Revelation shows that this idolatrous power is set in antithesis to another type. The great harlot of Revelation 17 is in contrast to the spotless bride of Revelation 19, and the idolatrous city of Revelation 18 is in contrast to the holy city of Revelation 21.

The Babylon of the Apocalypse seems undoubtedly an apostate religious system, linked with Papal Rome but obviously having a wider significance than the Roman Catholic Church. When Babylon was captured by the Medes and Persians, the leaders of the ancient religious system fled to Pergamum and the city became the headquarters of the old pagan religion and the king of Pergamum became the Pontifex Maximus. When Attalus III, the king of Pergamum, died in 133 B.C., he bequeathed to the citizens of Rome his royal and priestly offices, his dominions and his great wealth. Subsequently, the Babylonian initiates migrated from

Asia Minor to Italy, settling in the Etruscan plain, from whence they propagated the Etruscan Mysteries, which were precisely the same as those of the old cult. Eventually Rome became the centre and the Pontifex Maximus was established there. When Julius Caesar became the head of the state, he was elected Pontifex Maximus, and this title was held by each of the Roman emperors down to Gratian. The latter refused a title which made him the head of the State pagan religion and in 378 A.D., Damasus, the then bishop of Rome, was appointed Pontifex Maximus and became not only the head of the church of Rome, but also the legitimate successor of the old Babylonian pontiffs, with his pontificate extending over the pagans. The College of Cardinals is the counterpart of the pagan college of pontiffs, deriving from the original council at Babylon. The worship of the queen of heaven and her son, purgatorial purification after death, holy water, priestly absolution, dedicated virgins, reservation of all knowledge to the priesthood, unification of political and religious control, and many another feature of the ancient Babylonian system have been taken over and assimilated by Papal Rome. The significance of the name of Babylon, by which the future One World Church is described, is therefore obvious.

The vision of Babylon in Revelation 17 portrays her as a great harlot sitting upon a scarlet beast which had seven heads and ten horns and was 'full of names of blasphemy'. The identity of the beast is clear from Revelation 13 : 1–10; 17 : 10–14; Daniel 2 : 41–44, 7 : 7–11 and other prophecies : it is a federation of ten nations under the rule of one who later claims divine homage for himself (2 Thess. 2 : 4). Riding upon the beast the woman dominated the great apostate empire and was supported by its military and political might. Yet the true character of the beast is shown to be one of blatant and unashamed blasphemy. Arrayed in purple and scarlet (significantly the garments of popes and cardinals) and decked with gold and jewels, the woman held in her hand a golden cup full of her adulterous abominations and filthiness. As 2 Kings 23:13; Isaiah 44:19; Ezekiel 16:36, etc., indicate, abominations such as those which filled her cup are a symbol of idolatry. Rome's idolatry has always been productive of immorality, and the filth which filled the cup is comprised of all her encouragements to sin, indulgences, enforced celibacy, auricular confession, conventual life and so on.

As the common prostitute in olden times wore her name on her brow, so a name was impressed upon the forehead of the great whore: 'Mystery, Babylon the Great, the mother of harlots and of the abominations of the earth.' She is said to sit upon seven mountains and is finally identified in Revelation 17:18 as 'the great city, which has kingship over the kings of the earth'. Quite clearly, what is portrayed is a tremendous religious system, exercising authority over the political power, having its headquarters at Rome but being much larger in scope than Roman Catholicism since the woman is 'the mother of harlots'. The one-world church, for which so many are striving today, will inevitably be achieved in the future, but it is significant that the headquarters will remain at Rome. Reunion with Rome will be on Rome's terms and she is unlikely to offer any compromise.

The universal church of the future will evidently be in such close co-operation with the political power that her will is dominant and her supreme authority is acknowledged throughout the empire. Such a close association will patently have a considerable effect in binding the countries together in loyalty to the leader approved so wholeheartedly by the church. The period of ecclesiastical domination will, however, be strictly limited, for Daniel 9:27 indicates that, not long after the rise of this great western ruler and no more than three and a half years after the enactment of a treaty by him with Israel, he will put a stop to all religious observances throughout Israel and the ten nations and substitute for them the worship of himself and of his image in the temple at Jerusalem. Faithful witnesses to God will be martyred (Rev. 11:7) and the false church, Babylon the Great, will be destroyed (Rev. 17:16). There will possibly be other contributory factors. Obviously the church will not tolerate the rival claims made by the emperor, but additionally the constantly increasing wealth of the church will attract criticism. The western ruler and his satellite powers will apparently become restive under the church's intolerant sway and, coveting her wealth, will turn upon her and strip her of her wealth and treasures. Just as Henry VIII plundered the English churches and monasteries, so will this latter church suffer spoliation and destruction at the hand of the political power. It seems only fitting that the end of the great religious system should be due to the very powers which allowed her to exercise despotic control over the lives of their subjects.

Revelation 18 discloses that the fall of Babylon will have far-reaching effects. The vast commercial and economic system, which has brought—and will yet bring —nations and kingdoms into its toils, will suddenly collapse without warning. So complete will be its destruction that the Apocalypse depicts it as a mighty conflagration, which strikes fear into the hearts of the spectators. From every quarter will rise the wails from those whose temporal prosperity has been destroyed.

The details given show plainly that Babylon will be the personification of the commercial spirit as well as of the ecclesiastical, and there are already confirmatory evidences of this. The future of the one-world church, as portrayed in Scripture, may be summed up as a sudden rise to power, followed by an equally sudden fall. It is a false church and a mere counterfeit of the true. The success attending the efforts of men to produce a masterpiece of ecclesiastical unity will only facilitate the ultimate destruction of the great religious system.

In the light of the prophetic word, it is difficult to see how a true Christian can have any part in the building of a united church under the headship of Rome, incorporating conflicting loyalties and beliefs, composed of modernists and evangelicals, and regenerate and unregenerate and even extending a cloak over religions which do not acknowledge Christ at all. The unity of the true church is not organisational but spiritual, created and maintained by the Holy Spirit, and appropriate only to those who are members of the one body by faith in Christ and His atoning work. Any other form of unity is of human construction and not of divine origin. The Babylonian harlot produced by man's effort will be destroyed by the political power which she supported and dominated, but nothing can shake the fabric of the true church and even 'the gates of hell shall not prevail against it' (Matt. 16:18). If the formation of the false church now seems to be on the horizon, then the return of Christ for the true church cannot long be postponed.

6

EUROPEAN FEDERATION

As long ago as 1634 the Duc de Sully of France published, in *The Grand Design*, proposals for a federation of European states, governed by a senate of 66, nominated by the constituent states and, in 1948, Sir Winston Churchill significantly said at the Hague Congress, 'After this long passage of years, we are all servants of *The Grand Design*.' In 1930 the French Government submitted the proposals of Aristide Briand for a European federation of states, with a central body to deal with questions of tariffs, transport, finance, health, social welfare, technology, etc. Over the years repeated suggestions have been made with the objects of reducing the possibilities of war, abolishing tariff barriers, utilising resources to the full and eliminating unnecessary competition; but all efforts were unsuccessful until the second half of the twentieth century.

In 1957 six European countries (Belgium, France, Holland, Italy, Luxembourg and West Germany) signed two treaties at Rome, one of which established the European Economic Community (the E.E.C. or the Common Market, as it is usually termed) and the other the European Atomic Energy Community (or Euratom). These followed the setting up six years earlier of the European Coal and Steel Community (E.C.S.C.). Each of the three Communities originally had an executive body in the form of a Commission, but the three Commissions were merged into one on July 1st, 1967, and

Prof. Hallstein, who had been President for ten years, was then succeeded by M. Jean Rey, a leading Belgian statesman. The Communities themselves are also becoming one.

A Parliamentary Assembly, which came into being for the purposes of the E.C.S.C., was converted into a European Parliament, composed of 142 representatives drawn from the parliaments of the six participating countries. The legislative body, however, is not really the European Parliament, but the Council of Ministers, consisting of one representative from each country, although other Ministers are co-opted for discussion of their particular fields of responsibility : this facilitates direct contact with Departments of State in each country. The Commission is responsible for the initiation and implementation of policy and for ensuring the application of the provisions of the treaties. Proposals made by the Commission can be amended only by the unanimous vote of the Council and it has, therefore, a very considerable power, and its President has an authority and importance which are not usually realised. Article 189 of the treaty specifically states that regulations and directives issued by the Council and the Commission are binding upon the states which are members of the Community, and that any decisions taken are binding upon those to whom they are directed. In addition, there is a Court of Justice, located at Luxembourg, which was originally set up to deal with E.C.S.C. matters, but which is now concerned with all three Communities. Governments, firms and individuals, as well as the Commission, may bring cases before the Court, and its decisions are legally binding. Community Secretariats are concerned with specialist matters, one dealing, for example, solely with trade unions.

The aims and objects of the Economic Community are set out in Article 3 of the treaty as follows:

(*a*) the elimination, as between Member States, of customs duties and of quantitative restrictions in regard to the import and export of goods, as well as of all other measures having equivalent effect;

(*b*) the establishment of a common customs tariff and of a common commercial policy towards third countries;

(*c*) the abolition, as between Member States, of obstacles to the free movement of persons, services and capital;

(*d*) the inauguration of a common policy in the field of agriculture;

(*e*) the inauguration of a common policy in the field of transport;

(*f*) the establishment of a system ensuring that competition in the Common Market is not distorted;

(*g*) the adoption of procedures permitting the co-ordination of the economic policies of Member States and the correction of instability in their balances of payments;

(*h*) the approximation of their respective national laws to the extent required for the Common Market to function in an orderly manner;

(*i*) the creation of a European Social Fund in order to improve the possibilities of employment for workers and to contribute to the raising of their standard of living;

(*j*) the establishment of a European Investment Bank to facilitate the economic expansion of the Community by opening up fresh resources; and

(*k*) the association of overseas countries and territories with a view to increasing trade and to pursuing jointly the task of economic and social development.

It will be noted that these go far beyond mere questions of tariffs and cover an extremely wide field.

The benefits of the Community have been described as 'greater specialisation, less vulnerability to cyclical depressions ... cheaper goods, higher wages, more stable prices'. Mr. Harold MacMillan has rightly pointed out in *Britain, the Commonwealth and Europe*, 'in this new European Community, bringing together the manpower, the national resources and the inventive skills of some of the most advanced countries of the world, a new organisation is rapidly developing with the ability to stand on an equal footing with the great power groupings of the world' (i.e. the U.S.A., Russia and China). Already the Community covers 170 million people : the trade between the six countries amounts to £8,000 million a year, and imports from other countries to £10,000 million, and exports to other countries to £10,000 million. It is consequently the largest trading unit in the world.

One of the primary objects of the formation of the E.E.C. was to establish a common market between a number of European countries. This has involved the gradual abolition of all customs and import duties and trade barriers between the member countries, and on July 1st, 1968, the last tariffs disappeared. On the other hand, uniform tariffs are being fixed for imports from other countries into E.E.C. countries. For Britain, of course, the arrangements would mean the end of Imperial Preference to or by Commonwealth countries. No member state would be able to negotiate trade agreements on its own account. The negotiations would be by the Commission for the benefit of all members.

An essential to the success of the Community must inevitably be a fairly complete control of the commercial and industrial structure of the member states, and agreement on common economic and commercial policy. The greatest benefits of union can be achieved only if the production of particular goods or the manufacture of particular plant and machinery is concentrated in firms which are capable of the most economical and efficient production or manufacture, irrespective of the location of the firms. The capacity of other firms released in consequence of such concentration would then become available for other types of work, and central direction of industry and labour is clearly implicit. The elimination of duplication and inefficiency is practicable only if firms can be specifically instructed regarding the purpose for which their capacity is to be used. Complete industrial freedom is patently inconsistent with the rationalisation of production. The adoption of such a policy would facilitate the use of improved methods and mass production techniques, resulting in a larger scale of production and this should lead to a general reduction in prices.

One consequence of concentration, which is feared by many, is the necessity for the mobility of labour. If work of the kind for which they are specially trained is not available in their own locality, skilled workers may have to be either persuaded or directed to move to other localities or even other countries. The barriers to free movement were to be removed completely by the end of 1969, and any discrimination on grounds of nationality is already prohibited. Full social welfare benefits are to be provided by the six states for workers, irrespective of nationality. A European Social Fund has been set up to provide resettlement schemes and allowances for workers who have to move, and it is the intention that wage rates shall be aligned throughout the six countries. Because of labour shortages in certain fields, it has also been said that 'occupational mobility has become an essential complement to geographical mobility'. A similar mobility of capital is obviously an essential corollary of planned production, and all restrictions on such movements are being abolished. It is not difficult to envisage in the ultimate a complete centralisation of control of industry, with the Commission deciding, for example, the location of factories, the employment of labour, the best means of production and so on.

Article 240 of the Rome treaty sets no duration for the agreement and makes no provision for withdrawal and legally no member of the Community can sever its connection with the others. The organisation is permanent and the six member states are now virtually an entity.

Membership of the Community cannot be limited to economics. Prof. Hallstein, the President for ten years, emphasised on more than one occasion that the aim was political as well as economic union. 'We are not in business to promote tariff preferences,' he said. 'We are not in business at all: we are in politics.' Before the Rome treaties had been negotiated, the first session of the European Assembly at Strasbourg in September 1949 passed a resolution that 'The aim and goal is the creation of a European Political Authority, with limited functions but real powers.' When Britain made her second attempt to join the E.E.C., the statement of her case submitted to the Council of Ministers on July 4th, 1967, said, *inter alia*, 'We are aiming at something far more than material prosperity. We see this leading to greater political purpose for Western Europe. And if that purpose is to be realised, Britain must share it. We want, as soon as we can, to develop really effective political unity with our fellow West Europeans. . . . We believe that Europe can emerge as a Community expressing its own point of view, and exercising influence on world affairs, not only in the commercial and economic fields, but also in the political and defence fields. We shall play our full part in this process. Indeed it is a realisation of this European potential which has above all aroused our desire to join.' During the earlier negotiations of 1961–63, Mr. Edward Heath confirmed Britain's readiness to take part in political union, while Mr. Harold MacMillan, then Prime Minister, acknowledged that 'political unity is the central aim of these European countries and we would naturally accept that ultimate goal', and added that membership would involve 'a pooling of sovereignty by all concerned'. There is no doubt that ultimate political integration is inevitable and that member countries will have to sacrifice a considerable measure of national sovereignty to the supra-national authority.

The question of political co-operation has already been discussed at various levels. At a conference at Bad Godesburg on July 18th, 1961, it was decided, 'first, to organise political co-operation between the members of the Six on a regular basis, which would lead to the adoption of a common foreign policy; second, to hold further meetings of Heads of State or of Government at regular intervals in order to further the political unification of Europe and thus to strengthen the Atlantic Alliance; finally, a committee . . . was instructed to submit proposals to the Heads of State or of Government on ways and means which would make it possible to give a statutory character to the unification of their peoples.' In November 1961 the French Government submitted the draft of a treaty to establish a union of states to secure full co-operation in the fields of foreign policy, defence, science and culture. The proposals proved unacceptable but a revised French draft was discussed at Paris on April 17th, 1962. No agreement was reached at that meeting and the question has still to be resolved. It is acknowledged, however, that some form of political integration may well depend—as in the economic and industrial field—upon the Commission being given very considerable powers and upon the President being accorded virtually dictatorial authority in certain areas. It is not irrelevant that, to quote J. J. Ruddock, 'On the May 16th, 1960, a Parliamentary White Paper was circulated, which stated that H.M. Government was prepared to surrender its full sovereignty to a world government to be formed. The same day the U.S.A. and Italy made similar declarations. Since then nine other nations have made similar declarations.'

An interesting and significant feature of the Community is that 77 per cent of the population of the six countries are Roman Catholic and that the R.C. Church has a very great interest in these countries. A few years ago the magazine *Realities* said, 'Even more than industrial and banking circles, the Catholic circles of the six countries are prepared to unite their activities on a European scale, for they are backed by the Universal Church. It should be noted too that the Church was very active in bringing about a European Union of the six Common Market countries. . . . Just as banking and industry, concentrated along the Rhine and within the Hamburg–Geneva–Le Havre triangle, can hope to dominate economic activity through European union, the Church had a solid majority in the Common Market countries. . . . The co-ordination of European

Catholics is already taking place.... There is hardly any need to repeat the part which Catholicism plays in the political life of Europe. It supports political parties of all six countries: the C.D.U. in Germany, the M.R.P. in France, the Christian Democratic Party in Italy, the Social Christian Party in Belgium, and the People's Catholic Party in the Netherlands.' Such a strong religious influence can scarcely be ignored.

The picture which is rapidly forming in Europe has certain significant colours. There is already a fairly close-knit Community, which is evidently destined to become either a union or a federation of states, economically, commercially and politically. Commerce, industry, labour and finance are coming under the control of a central authority. It seems inevitable that national sovereignty will be surrendered, either wholly or partly to a supra-national power. A bias is evident towards dictatorship rather than true democracy. A strong Roman Catholic influence is prevalent. These details are of considerable interest and naturally raise the question whether any reflection of them or of the Community itself is discoverable in Biblical prophecy.

Dogmatism in matters of this kind is singularly inappropriate, but it may be no coincidence that the Book of Revelation does describe the formation, in the latter days, of a political union of ten countries (Rev. 13), and Daniel 2 and 7 make it clear that this federation appears on the world's stage not long before the return of the Lord Jesus Christ to earth in power and glory to establish a theocratic kingdom. From the Old Testament passages, it may perhaps be deduced that the predicted federation has a relationship (presumably, at least in part, geographical) with the old Roman Empire, although it is evident from the descriptions given that it is not of the same character. It may be deduced from

Revelation 18 that, despite the advantage of political union, the purpose of the ten states in joining together will not be restricted to this, but will also be for the purpose of securing commercial benefits as well. The chapter indicates that producers and merchants will enjoy the utmost prosperity through the union of the countries and that many will be enriched through the great system. The picture is certainly not dissimilar to the normal expectation on the Continent of Common Market developments. Nor is it perhaps irrelevant that a great deal of the area of the old Roman Empire is covered by the member states of the European Community.

From the federated ten countries, prophecy discloses that a powerful ruler will emerge, who will be completely ruthless, merciless and atheistic. His career will evidently commence with the subjugation of three countries (Dan. 7:8), after which seven other nations will surrender their sovereignty to him (Rev. 17:13). Europe today needs a leader of strength and personality and it is not infeasible that, if such a man arose who had proved his ability in the organisation and unification of three other countries, the Community would be prepared to accept his leadership. Reference is made in Daniel 9:27 to a treaty between this ruler and Israel—a possible indication that, for the first time, an individual had arisen with the ability to solve the Middle East problem. This, however, is speculation, but the Bible does paint the picture of a supreme dictator, to whose direction all industry and labour will be subject, no one being able to trade (or 'buy or sell') except with his permission (Rev. 13:16, 17).

The anticipated development of central control in the European Community is remarkably similar to what was predicted in the Apocalypse 19 centuries ago.

Indeed, in October 1957, Henri Spaak, who was then Secretary General of N.A.T.O., said in Paris, 'We do not want another committee; we have too many already. What we want is a man of sufficient stature to hold the allegiance of all people and to lift us out of the economic morass into which we are sinking. Send us such a man and be he god or devil, we will receive him.'

This mighty ruler of the future will apparently be under the influence for a period of a great religious organisation, depicted as a prostitute under the name of Babylon the Great. The Apocalypse portrays this evil character as an adulteress and a murderess and declares that she will sit upon seven mountains and that she is a great city reigning over the kings of the earth (Rev. 17:6, 9, 18). Rome has often been termed the seven-hilled city and many commentators have taken the view that the religious system described as Babylon is clearly identifiable with the Roman Catholic Church (although possibly of a far more extensive character than at present), which has consistently claimed both political and ecclesiastical sovereignty. It is not without significance that three quarters of the population of the E.E.C. countries is Roman Catholic, and that the R.C. Church does exercise a tremendous influence in the affairs of those countries.

So far as the prophetic word is concerned, Revelation 17:16, 17 indicates that the political power of the future will eventually turn upon the great religious organisation and completely destroy it, only to discover that the downfall of the ecclesiastical body will result in irreparable commercial loss. All the merchants, traders and mariners, who had profited so extensively from the activities of the system, will wail over the losses which they will consequently suffer (Rev. 18).

The destruction of the ecclesiastical power will evidently be the preliminary step to the resurrection of the old Caesar worship, since the mighty western dictator will claim worship as God (2 Thess. 2:4). This may seem incredible, but Revelation 13:15 discloses that his diabolically endued confederate will impart life and breath to the inanimate image of the dictator. At this supernatural occurrence the world will pay its homage to a man. These events may not be very remote.

It would be foolish to maintain dogmatically, as some have done, that the Common Market, or the European Community, is to be identified with a revived Roman Empire or with the federation of ten kingdoms of which prophecy speaks. On the other hand, it is certainly clear that an extraordinary resemblance exists between the prophetic picture and that which is at present being painted before our eyes. The similarity is, in fact, so marked that we may well be seeing today the initial stages in the formation of the great Western power which is to appear after the translation of the church from this scene. If the fulfilment of prophecy seems to be looming up, then one must again conclude that the return of our Lord for His church cannot be far distant.

7

THE JEWISH SIGN

TODAY'S problem of the Middle East virtually originated in an act of faithlessness 4,000 years ago, when Sarah attempted to secure the fulfilment of a Divine promise by carnal methods (Gen. 15:3; 16:2). Through her misguided action, two races came into being who were destined to disturb the world. For Abraham had two sons, one born of an Egyptian servant, and the other born 14 years later of his wife. It was impossible for the home to hold the two and, in consequence of Ishmael's mockery at his brother's weaning, Hagar and he were cast out, to take up their residence eventually in the wilderness of Paran, to the south of Canaan. Ishmael subsequently married an Egyptian (Gen. 21:21) and, as God had foretold (Gen. 17:26), became the father of 12 princes as well as of one daughter who later married his nephew Esau (Gen. 36:3).

· Before Hagar's son was born, God promised, 'I will multiply thy seed exceedingly, that it shall not be numbered for multitude' (Gen. 16:10), and He later declared that He would make Ishmael a great nation (Gen. 17:20; 21:18). To Isaac, God promised specific territorial possessions (Gen. 26:3, 4), but no pledge of this kind was made to Ishmael. As foretold, the latter's descendants multiplied very quickly and they inhabited the greater part of Northern Arabia, from the borders of Egypt to the Gulf of Aqabah (Gen. 25:18). The majority were nomadic in character and dwelt in camps, but some became merchants and settled down in walled cities.

By a specific covenant with Abraham, God bestowed the land of Canaan upon his seed as an everlasting possession, and subsequently assured him that the chosen seed was not Ishmael but Isaac (Gen. 17:8; 21:12). Although Israel's entitlement to the land is today strongly disputed by the Arab, the Divine pledge was quite specific and unambiguous, and it must eventually be implemented.

History repeated itself in Isaac's case, and like his father he had two sons with little love for one another. Because of Esau's murderous hatred, Jacob (or Israel) made his home for some 20 years in Padan-Aram in Mesopotamia, before returning to Canaan and finally to spend 17 years in Egypt. Esau settled in the area of Mount Seir, on the plateau running from the Dead Sea to the Gulf of Aqabah. The original inhabitants of Seir were the Horites and Esau (or Edom as he became known) added to his wives a Horite princess, but it was not long before his descendants, the Edomites, had completely destroyed or absorbed the Horites (Deut. 2:12-22).

The hatred between the brothers was transmitted to their posterity and centuries later Ezekiel's prophecy referred to it as 'a perpetual hatred' (Ezek. 35:5). It has been evidenced repeatedly in history. When, for example, the Israelites left Egypt to make their way to Canaan, they sought permission to pass through Edom, but the latter quite unreasonably refused them entry (Num. 20:14-21). David brought the Edomites into subjection (2 Sam. 8:14; 1 Kings 11:15, 16), but they still remained a thorn in the side of Israel. When, later, Nebuchadnezzar destroyed Jerusalem and carried Judah away captive, the Edomites in their mountain fastnesses not only lifted no finger to help God's people but, delighting in the troubles of their neighbours, seized the opportunity of taking possession of the southern part of Judah and, as Dr. Clyde Harrington says, thereby 'intensified the already smouldering hatred between the Jews and the Edomites' (see Psa. 137:7; Ezek. 25:12–14; Amos 1:11; Obad. 10–14). The Edomites were never afterwards driven out of the land. Under the Persian régime, Edom became a province of the Persian Empire under the name of Idumea (the Greek form of Edom).

Israel, Ishmael and Edom were all descendants of Abraham, but this common ancestry has produced animosity rather than fraternal affection. Ishmael's hatred of the Jew dates back to God's selection of Isaac in preference to Ishmael. Edom's antagonism is due to his supersession by Jacob. The Edomites and the Ishmaelites were close neighbours, occupying adjoining country and intermingling with each other. G. F. Owen says, 'The peoples throughout this region so managed their interests, married and intermarried, that the Ishmaelites, Edomites, Midianites, Horites, Amalekites, Ammonites, Moabites and other cognate tribes, became known as the "Westerners" or "Arabs"—those who lived in or adjacent to the Wady el Arabah.... Today we know them as the "Maadites", or Northern Arabs.' The Himyarites, who inhabited Southern Arabia or, the Yemen, and the Maadites were ultimately fused into one people. In 325 B.C. the Nabatean Arabs (descendants of Nebaioth, Ishmael's eldest son) swept over eastern Idumea, taking possession of Petra, and within the next two or three centuries it became difficult to distinguish between the descendants of Ishmael and those of Edom, although Idumea still remained as a province when the Romans took over Palestine. Antipater, the father of Herod the Great and procurator of

Judea, was an Idumean. The modern Arab probably owes something to both Ishmael and Edom.

In the sixth century B.C. Cyrus authorised the Jews throughout the Persian Empire to return to Palestine, to rebuild the temple and to restore the Levitical rites and ceremonies.

When the Messiah came His people were, therefore, in the land, but they rejected Him and God consequently gave them up. In A.D. 70 Jerusalem and the temple were destroyed by the Roman army and, after Bar Cochba's rebellion in A.D. 134, the Jews were banished from Jerusalem and forbidden to approach the city. They gradually drifted back, however, and lived in comparative peace among both Christians and Arabs.

In the early part of the seventh century, Mohammed, who claimed descent from Ishmael, succeeded in bringing under his control the wild tribes of Arabia, and within ten years of his death in A.D. 632 his followers had established a great Moslem empire, ruled from Damascus. In A.D. 637 the Caliph Omar took Jerusalem and a few decades later the first Dome of the Rock was built on the temple site. The Moslem empire lasted—with the exception of 90 years of Crusaders' rule and 270 years by the Mamelukes of Egypt—until A.D. 1517, when Palestine fell into the hands of the Turks and remained part of the Ottoman Empire for four centuries.

Despite the fact of Israel's conquest of Canaan nearly three and a half millennia ago and of the long history of their occupation of that country, it is perhaps not unnatural that the Arabs—as the more recent inhabitants—should consider that they have some claim to Palestine. Nor can one ignore the Divine promise that Ishmael should be a great nation—although this gives no entitlement to the land specifically promised to Israel.

Through the four centuries of the Turkish régime, Arabs and Jews lived side by side, both chafing under the foreign yoke and yearning for the day when they could throw off the fetters and take unhindered possession of Palestine again. When Turkey entered the First World War on September 8th, 1914, Britain was well aware of the Arab feeling and at once conveyed to them an offer of financial assistance if they rose against the Turks and joined the Allies. The Arabs informed Sir Henry McMahon (the British High Commissioner for Egypt) that the price of their co-operation was the political independence of the Arab countries. They defined the eastern boundaries, but inadvertently omitted any reference to any western boundary—an omission which was one of the principal causes of subsequent misunderstanding. Their desired independence was guaranteed and, accepting the McMahon pledge, the Arabs revolted against Turkey. Largely through the efforts of T. E. Lawrence, an army of 200,000 Bedouin was enlisted and this took an active part in harassing and demoralising the Turks.

Over 20 years before this, an Austrian Jew named Theodor Herzl, a doctor of law of Vienna University, who had left the legal profession to become a press reporter, was sent by his newspaper to Paris to report on the changes which had occurred following the French Revolution. Among other things, he witnessed and reported on the trial of Capt. Alfred Dreyfus, who was convicted of treason and sentenced to imprisonment. Herzl was convinced that Dreyfus was innocent and that he had been made a scapegoat because he was a Jew.

The trial gave the Austrian reporter a new purpose in life and in 1895 he published a small volume, entitled *The Jewish State*, presenting a case for settlement of

Jews in Palestine. The following year he met Dr. William Heckler, a Hebrew Christian employed in the British Embassy at Vienna, and his new acquaintance gave him a copy of a book which he himself had published, entitled *The Return of the Jews to Palestine in Accordance with Prophecy*. Dr. Heckler's book made a tremendous impression upon Herzl, and its author seems to have convinced him that settlement of the Jews in Palestine was not only clearly predicted in the Bible but was also specifically pledged by God. Herzl had planned a Zionist Congress at Basle in 1897 with the object of arousing Jews to a realisation of their destiny and of securing their active support to the case for a Jewish home in Palestine, and he invited Heckler (although a Christian) to speak at the Congress. This Congress was the real origin of the Zionist Movement and although its founder never saw the fruits of his labours, the existence in Palestine of a State of Israel today is an indication of the success of his initial efforts.

In 1904 another strong supporter of Zionism, Dr. Chaim Weizmann, a professor of the University of Geneva, left Switzerland to take up an appointment in Britain at Victoria University, Manchester. Weizmann was active in the cause of the Jewish race and while lecturing to chemistry students at the university, he continued to prosecute the aims of Zionism to the full. When it was suggested that Uganda should be offered for the settlement of the Jews, it was Weizmann who made it clear to Mr. A. J. Balfour that the proposal was completely unacceptable and that nothing less than Palestine would satisfy Jewish aspirations and hopes. When the First World War broke out, Weizmann was professor of medical chemistry at the university, but was actively engaged in securing support for a Hebrew university in Palestine. Among those whose sympathy he enlisted for the project were Baron Edmond de Rothschild, Mr. James de Rothschild, Dr. Paul Ehrlich, Prof. Otto Warburg and other leading personalities in the financial and academic fields. His primary interest in the settlement of Jews in Palestine, however, received unexpected encouragement in consequence of the war.

Early in the war, Britain found it impossible to obtain an adequate supply of wood alcohol for the production of acetone, which was used as a solvent in cordite and was sorely needed for the manufacture of explosives. When he first came to Manchester, Weizmann had engaged in research into the production of synthetic acetone from starch and, at the request of the government, he now undertook the task of developing the process and building factories for large-scale production. His services to the country in this respect were of such outstanding value that it was proposed to bestow an honour upon him. But the Swiss professor declined the offer and asked instead for a home for the Jew in Palestine. Objections were made by the Pope, by France, and even by certain influential Jews in Britain, but in the end Weizmann realised his ambition and Mr. A. J. Balfour, who was then Foreign Secretary, addressed the following letter to Lord Rothschild on behalf of the government on November 2nd, 1917:

'I have much pleasure in conveying to you, on behalf of His Majesty's Government, the following declaration of sympathy with Jewish Zionist aspirations, which has been submitted to, and approved by, the Cabinet.

'His Majesty's Government view with favour the establishment in Palestine of a national home for the Jewish people, and will use their best endeavours to facilitate the achievement of this object, it being clearly understood that nothing shall be done which may prejudice the civil and religious rights of existing non-Jewish communities in Palestine, or the rights and political status enjoyed by Jews in any other country.

'I should be grateful if you would bring this declaration to the knowledge of the Zionist Federation.'

As Paul Goodman says in his *History of the Jews*, 'The Balfour Declaration (as this communication came to be termed) was hailed by the Jews all over the world as an act of national liberation comparable to the decree of Cyrus of Persia which led to the re-establishment of the Jewish Commonwealth in Judea after the Babylonian Captivity.' The Arabs were stunned. It had been their clear impression that the McMahon pledge to Emir Hussein of Mecca was that the whole of Palestine (although not actually mentioned) should be theirs. Although Britain maintained that this was never intended, the Arabs were bitter in their denunciation of the British action. Early in 1917 a commission of four British and four French members, headed by Dr. Chaim Weizmann, was appointed by the government to plan the implementation of the Balfour Declaration. In Palestine, Weizmann consulted everyone who might be concerned and discussed proposals with Arabs and British and so impressed General Allenby by his earnestness and singleness of purpose that the General was almost converted to Zionism.

In 1920 a compromise was accepted, as a result of which Feisal (one of Hussein's four sons) became Emir of Jordan, but this did not ease the situation very much. Although initially the Arabs got on quite well with the few Jews in Palestine at that time, tempers soon began to fray and it was quite clear that no reconciliation of the Balfour declaration and the McMahon pledge could be found that would satisfy the Arabs. Since the problem seemed temporarily insoluble, Palestine was declared to be a mandated territory in 1922 and the mandate was awarded to Britain, the Balfour declaration (which had already been incorporated into the Treaty of Sèvres) being embodied in the mandate. Article 2 of the mandate stipulated that 'the Mandatory shall be responsible for placing the country under such political, administrative and economic conditions as will secure the establishment of the Jewish national home'.

The active hostility of the Arabs soon made itself felt and atrocities of the most brutal character were committed. Over a period of nearly three decades, White Papers galore were issued, the problem was investigated by individuals and by various bodies, every possible proposal was made, but all to no avail: the only effect was to exacerbate feelings. The views of the Jews and the Arabs were completely irreconcilable.

A few years after, an entirely new factor was introduced in Adolf Hitler. If the Jewish people had suffered pogroms and persecutions in the past, these tribulations were completely eclipsed by their experiences in the Central Europe of the twentieth century. The Nazi policy was clearly complete genocide, and for the majority of Jews in Europe escape seemed impossible.

The national home in Palestine seemed a will-o'-the-wisp, although numbers did, in fact, find their way there. Arab opposition to the influx of Jews flared up into a revolt which was quelled with difficulty, but armed bands of guerillas continued to attack the Jews. The Haganah, an underground army of Jewish volunteers, rose up to defend themselves and the terrorist organisation of the Irgun Zvai Leumi took full revenge on the Arabs for any injury suffered. The inevitable imposition by Britain of restrictions on immigration was bitterly resented by the Jews and, after the Second World War, Jewish terrorism and sabotage added their quota to the unrest created by Arab violence.

Finding the situation too difficult to cope with, in 1947 Britain referred the whole matter to the U.N., who eventually proposed the ending of the mandate and the partition of the country. The result was an immediate outbreak of violence by the Arabs. Determined to put an end to her responsibilities, Britain announced that the mandate would be terminated on May 14th, 1948, and on that day the Union Jack was lowered and the High Commissioner departed, leaving the Jews to their fate.

The same day, Mr. David Ben Gurion, the Premier elect, proclaimed the establishment of the Jewish State of Israel, and Dr. Chaim Weizmann became the first President of Israel.

There seemed little hope of the survival of the new state. From all sides the Arabs attacked. The forces of Egypt, Jordan, Syria, Lebanon, Iraq and Saudi-Arabia descended upon Israel with the avowed intention of exterminating the Jews. But, to the amazement of the world, the little nation of 650,000 routed the armies of the opposing nations of 40 million people. The armistice signed in 1949 resulted in an uneasy peace, with sporadic outbreaks of trouble and border skirmishes. Arab infiltrators stole Jewish produce and equipment, dynamited buildings, destroyed property and massacred Jews. The Arab nations imposed an economic blockade on the little state, and Egypt banned Israeli ships through Suez and cut off entrance to the Gulf of Aqabah.

In 1956 Egypt, Syria and Jordan formed a unified army command for the purpose of war on Israel, and Iraqi forces began massing on the Jordanian border. In October, Israel mobilised her army and, without waiting to be attacked, crossed into Sinai to break up the

Egyptian camps and to destroy the bases of terrorist gangs who were operating against Israel. In a few days the Jewish forces destroyed two Egyptian divisions and held most of the Sinai Peninsula. But for the cease fire enforced by the U.N., Egypt would have suffered a far more devastating defeat. It was not a victory won by military superiority or by brilliant strategy, however. As in 1948 a miracle occurred and a Divine hand intervened.

The bitterness felt by Egypt at her humiliating defeat made a further attack on Israel inevitable and Radio Cairo repeatedly declared, 'We are getting ready for the decisive battle and at the right moment we will strike with power and speed. All our coming battles with Israel will be battles of life or death.' Over a million Arab refugees in the Lebanon, Syria and Jordan, for whom repatriation and compensation had been repeatedly demanded, provided those countries with ample justification for war. The Jewish and Arab actions regarding the waters of the Jordan gave further provocation. Equipped by Russia with arms, tanks and aircraft, the Arab states were all prepared in 1967 to wipe out the Israeli state and when the outburst came, it seemed that nothing could save the little country. The Arabs had two and a half times as many armoured cars and three times as many military aircraft as the Israeli forces, and there was no possibility of help from any other country. A thousand Egyptian and Arab planes could have been in the air, bombing the cities of Israel and laying the land waste before any warning had been given, but they remained on the ground for Jewish bombers to destroy. The Arabs were driven back in disarray and for a third time in two decades, Israel was victorious. This was no mere accident, nor was it attributable merely to the ability and tenacity of the Jew.

The evidence once again leads to an inescapable conclusion. For a third time a miracle had occurred: God
had intervened.

But why should God be interested in these people
and their country? Nearly 4,000 years ago He entered
into a covenant with their ancestor Abraham, under
which He pledged the land of Canaan, from the river of
Egypt to the river Euphrates, to the patriarch's descendants as a permanent possession (Gen. 15:18–21;
17:7, 8). The covenant was unconditional and irrevocable and, as the apostle Paul plainly declared in Gala-
tions 3:17, the provisions could not be annulled by anything which occurred subsequently. The nation's sin
may have brought them under the Divine displeasure
and they may have had to suffer for their wrongdoing,
but God has not cast them off (Rom. 11:2, 25). Nothing
can alter His pledge or bring Israel's history to a close
(Isa. 54:10; Jer. 31:35, 36). He foresaw His people's
failure, but, despite their centuries-old apostasy from
Him, He confirmed that they would yet dwell in the
land He had promised and hold it as a permanent possession (Ezek. 37:25–28). That promise has not yet been
fulfilled and there is, therefore, clearly a future for
Israel.

When the Lord Jesus Christ entered the world, 'He
came unto His own, and His own received Him not'
(John 1:11). The Jews rejected Him and clamoured for
His death. They have suffered for centuries in consequence, wandering the face of the earth, harried and
harassed, persecuted and down-trodden. Not until the
present century has there again been a Jewish state in
Palestine—a land which every Jew can now call 'home'.

In the meantime God has ignored national and racial
distinctions and has been calling out a church, composed of Jews and Gentiles and united inseparably with

His Son. When this work has been finished, James declared that the words of Amos 9:11, 12 would be applicable. 'God at the first did visit the Gentiles, to take out of them a people for His name,' he acknowledged, but 'after this I will return and will build again the ruins thereof, and I will set it up: that the residue of men might seek after the Lord' (Acts 15:16, 17). In other words, when the church era ends, God will proceed to fulfil His pledge to Israel. Our Lord foretold that Jerusalem would 'be trodden down of the Gentiles until the times of the Gentiles be fulfilled' (Luke 21:24). For the first time since He uttered the words, the city of Jerusalem is today held by Israel and no longer by the Gentiles, and although the city has still to suffer the ravages of war and to be 'trodden down' again, the end times now seem to be casting their shadow before.

Centuries ago God declared that He would scatter Israel among the heathen, from one end of the earth to the other, that they would find no rest for the sole of their foot and that they would constantly fear for their life. Yet He would not cast them away nor destroy them completely, but would eventually have compassion on them and gather them out of the nations and restore them to their own land (Lev. 26:33–39; Deut. 28:64–67; 30:1–5). Ezekiel predicted that one day God would bring His people into their land to till the desolate places and to demonstrate that He is their God (Ezek. 36:22–36). The assurance is definite: 'they shall dwell in the land that I have given unto Jacob my servant, wherein your fathers have dwelt; and they shall dwell therein, even they, and their children, and their children's children for ever' (Ezek. 37:25). Although those who have returned to Israel during the twentieth century have largely done so in unbelief, Jehovah will one day make Himself known among them and will restore the multitude of Israel to the land and to Himself.

Before that day of blessing comes, however, the land is to be deluged in blood. It is evident from Daniel 11:36–39 that the country will suffer the rule of a strong dictator, who is an apostate Jew and a servant of spirit forces. Revelation 13:12–17 indicates that this man will be in close alliance with another great political power—the great western ruler over ten nations, referred to in Daniel 7:23–25; 9:27; Revelation 13:1–8, etc.—to whom he seeks to direct the worship of the nations by the erection of an image of the ruler in the temple at Jerusalem and by the impartation of life to the image (Rev. 13:14, 15; 2 Thess. 2:3, 4). Our Lord long ago warned those living at that time, when they saw that sign, to flee to the mountains, for the ensuing period would be one of unparalleled tribulation (Matt. 24:16–22).

The Jewish victory of 1967 is not the last chapter in the story and a further military clash sooner or later is inevitable. A bitter hostility and a burning desire for revenge can only lead to an attack upon Israel by Egypt and her associates. Centuries ago, however, Psalm 83, referring to the enemies of God's people, said, 'They have said, Come and let us cut them off from being a nation; that the name of Israel may be no more in remembrance' and, detailing the confederated powers opposing Israel, the Psalmist included the Edomites, Ishmaelites, Moabites, Hagarenes, Gebal, Ammonites, Amalekites, Philistines, Tyrians and Assyrians. In *Egypt in Biblical Prophecy*, Dr. Wilbur M. Smith points out that ten nations are again listed by Isaiah as destined for judgment, viz., Babylon, Philistia, Moab, Damascus, Ethiopia, Egypt, Dumah (i.e. Edom), Arabia, the Valley of Vision and Tyre. Jeremiah also contains denunciations upon several of the same nations. Even earlier, Balaam foretold (Num. 24) the judgment of the Moabites, Edomites, Amalekites, Kenites, Assyrians and the descendants of Eber (i.e. the inhabitants of Southern Arabia, Ammonites, Moabites, etc.). It is significant that the peoples named occupied lands now possessed by Arabs and were themselves largely of the same stock. The future conflict and its outcome were, therefore, plainly portrayed in Biblical prophecy centuries ago. Israel will unquestionably suffer a full-scale attack by the Arab countries—possibly in the near future—but the God of Israel will deliver her and will defeat all her foes.

Daniel 11 discloses that Israel may expect further trouble from the south and an invasion by whirlwind attack from the north (presumably from Russia), the mighty hordes sweeping through to pillage and loot Egypt (Dan. 11:40–44). The resultant carnage and devastation are painted vividly in many of the Psalms. Despite the intervention of Israel's western ally, Zechariah declares that the Lord 'will make Jerusalem a cup of trembling unto all the people round about, when they shall be in the siege' and that He will 'make Jerusalem a burdensome stone for all people: all that burden themselves with it shall be cut in pieces, though all the people of the earth be gathered together against it' (Zech. 12:2, 3).

As if these troubles were not enough, there is an indication in Revelation 16:12 of an invasion from the Far East to add to all the tribulations of the little country. If Israel's woes have been great in the past, those awaiting her in the future are incomparably greater. Never has a nation suffered as much as the 'chosen nation' will have suffered.

Yet the Scriptures make it clear that nothing will

frustrate the Divine purposes for that nation. At the height of her calamities, when nations are gathered to battle, Jerusalem captured and pillaged, its women raped and its inhabitants carried captive, the Lord will suddenly descend to the city to destroy His people's foes and to sweep Israel clean of her invaders (Zech. 14:1–3; Rev. 19:11–16). He will come, not only to deliver His people, but to fulfil the age-long promises of their blessing. By His power, the people will be regathered from all quarters and settled in their own land (Ezek. 28:25, 26; Amos 9:14, 15; Zeph. 3:20): the nation will be spiritually regenerated (Rom. 11:26, 27; Jer. 23:6; 31:33, 34) and, no longer blind, will acknowledge Jehovah as their God (Zech. 13:9).

The land promised to Abraham will then be inherited by his descendants. Its topography will be altered and a fertile plain will replace the mountainous terrain (Zech. 14:4, 8–10). An abundance of rain will water the earth (Joel 2:23, 24) and the once-barren countryside transformed into a fertile field (Isa. 29:17). God will dwell in Zion, and Jerusalem will be a holy city, the centre of His government (Joel 3:17; Mic. 4:7). Representatives of the nations will be compelled to attend the feast of tabernacles each year in Jerusalem (Zech. 14:16) and the city will be the political centre of the earth. All the prophecies of a kingdom, age of blessing and prosperity will be fulfilled, and Israel will be supreme above the nations of the earth. There is a glorious future awaiting the Jew.

There are indications in current events that the days so long foretold cannot be far distant. The countries of the west are beginning to come together, a further attack from Egypt is expected before long; an intervention then from Russia seems inevitable; the threat from the Far East is slowly materialising; nearly 2½ million

Jews are already in the land and Israel is a state once again. The stage is set and the shadows of the actors are seen in the wings: soon the play will commence. But *before then*, the church of believing Christians will have been translated from this scene at the Coming of Christ (1 Thess. 4 : 15–17). If the fulfilment of prophecy seems imminent, the rapture of the church may be about to take place. Until that happens, the Divine plan for Israel is held in abeyance, but all the indications suggest that its implementation cannot long be postponed.

8

SOVIET RUSSIA

ALTHOUGH, in many respects, later to develop than most of her neighbours, Russia is now without question the most powerful nation in Europe. Over the centuries —and particularly from the sixteenth to the nineteenth —she gradually expanded until she attained imperial proportions, covering many races and spreading right across Asia to the Pacific. But it has been during the twentieth century that she has reached her present position of dominance.

Her ecclesiastical history is also interesting. The primitive religions to which her peoples originally paid allegiance were slowly superseded by Hellenistic Christianity, but when Constantinople was taken by the Turks in 1453, the Russian Church claimed that the 'heresies' of Rome and the overthrow of the Byzantine Empire left her as the major champion of the faith and the legitimate successor to Rome and Constantinople. Moscow accordingly styled herself 'the third Rome'. In 1589 her full autonomy was evidenced by the creation of an independent Russian patriarchate, although this independence only facilitated the ultimate subordination of the Church to the autocratic power of the Czar.

The overthrow of the imperial régime 50 years ago had serious repercussions on the Church. The latter was distrusted by the new order because it had been so completely under the control of the Czar, but it was also, as one writer puts it, 'an integral part of the despised and hated order from which Communism was emancipating mankind'. Karl Marx had described religion as 'the opium of the people'. To quote Prof. K. S. Latourette, 'Religion was deemed a convenient instrument of the exploiting classes for the maintenance of their privileged position. By it the proletariat was induced ... to endure misery and injustice in this life in the hope of consolation beyond the grave.' All church properties were confiscated by the state and a control was instituted over all religious activities. Atheism was officially propagated and a Union of the Godless was established which soon had a membership of several millions. Although a more tolerant attitude is alleged to prevail today, religious freedom is more nominal than real, and the state is still atheistic. Under Statutes 142 and 227 of the Soviet Criminal Code, anyone (whether parents or other persons) instructing minors in religion is liable to four years' imprisonment.

Nevertheless, it is impossible not to be impressed by the amazing development of the country over the last few decades. At the commencement of the present century, Russia was little more than a nation of serfs: today she has industrial, scientific and engineering achievements to her credit of which any country could justifiably be proud. What the U.S.S.R. has already done in space exploration, to take only one example, is simply remarkable, and it seems by no means unlikely that she will eventually outstrip America in the race for the lead in interplanetary flight. It is sometimes argued that her advance in rocketry and telemetry, for example, are due to the Russian armies having reached Berlin before the Allies did and carrying off the ablest German scientists, but this is not entirely true.

From a military point of view also, she is to be respected—if not feared—since her stockpile of nuclear weapons and ballistic missiles is almost undoubtedly equivalent to that of the U.S.A. She has now 1,350 inter-continental ballistic missiles and is adding 250 a year. Her 220 SS-9s can carry one 25 megaton warhead or three 5 megaton warheads. She has also developed a metallic radar chaff, which forms an impenetrable curtain and blinds any radar. In addition, Russia is developing a fractional orbit bombardment system that will enable her to send weapons or bombs into orbit at 100 miles' altitude and then to plunge into America viâ the Pole. Anti-ballistic missiles are no longer a defence against a sophisticated attack and, as one writer points out, 'the missile swarms that Russia could unleash—complete with multiple warheads, decoys and other penetration aids—would quickly swamp any defence system that the U.S. could realistically employ'. Fortunately Russia's idea of effecting world revolution by the use of any available means (not excluding war) has been partially superseded by the attempt to demonstrate the advantages of Communism (and the desirability, therefore, for revolution on the part of other peoples by their own effort) by the superiority, efficiency and general success of the Soviet state. But this does not rule out military action if, at any time, Russia deems it to be in her interest.

Lest one should be blinded by achievements, it is important to realise the aims and objects of the Russian ideology of Communism, and it should perhaps be traced to its origin. In 1185 a secret society was founded in France under the name of the *Confrérie de la Paix*, or Brotherhood of Peace. It was a pacifist movement, the primary object of which was to put an end to all wars, but among its avowed aims were also the abolition of religion, the overthrow of governments, ownership of all land by the people, the severing of marital ties, etc.

Three centuries later, in 1492, a new organisation appeared in Spain, the members of which called themselves *alumbrados*. This movement, which had very similar objects to those of the earlier French society, spread to France in 1623, but was suppressed three years later. It is obvious that it merely went underground since it reappeared in a slightly different form a century and a half later, principally through the efforts of a German named Adam Weishaupt, who was Professor of Canon Law at Ingolstadt. Weishaupt had previously dabbled in occultism and Satanism, and he now launched into an attack on governments, patriotism, family and social ties, and religion. On May 1st, 1776, he founded a secret society (said to have some connection with the Jesuits as well as with the organisations already mentioned above) called the Illuminati, the main object of which was world revolution. Illuminism aimed, however, not only at the overthrow of all governments, but also at the abolition of religion, the jettisoning of matrimonial ties and their supersession by free love, the communal education of children, the abolition of private ownership of property and so on. The Jacobin Club, from which the terrors of the French Revolution emanated, was organised by Weishaupt's disciples and adopted the same principles. Cagliostro, Robespierre, Mirabeau and others were among the more eminent Illuminati, and there is no doubt that the movement was largely responsible for the French Revolution in 1789.

In his *Proofs of a World Conspiracy*, published in 1797, Prof. John Robison states that Weishaupt was a Freemason and that he selected from the Masonic Lodge those members whom he thought most suitable and constituted them disciples of Illuminism, thus forming an association within the fold of Freemasonry, although distinct from it. Robison also traces the link between the new Order and the Jesuits. Justin McCarthy declares that 'the Illuminati were to overthrow the thrones of Europe. The first blow was to be struck in France. After the fall of the French monarchy, it was proposed to attack Rome. The society was said to have countless followers. It was said to possess enormous funds.' Why the French Revolution (which was obviously intended as the prototype for other revolutions) was not followed by similar action in other countries is still a perplexity to students of history.

Little was heard of the society for four or five decades, although there are evidences that it had by no means been dissolved or destroyed. The teachings of Illuminism reappeared in the nineteenth century in the writings of Karl Marx, a Prussian who was born a Jew and baptised a Christian, but who grew up to become an atheist. He and Friedrich Engels were banished from Germany as dangerous revolutionaries. In 1847, however, they joined the Communist League in Brussels, and in the following year Marx produced the *Communist Manifesto*. Marx maintained that the private ownership of property was the root of all evil, and he saw no possibility of any improvement in the condition of the proletariat short of a complete economic and political revolution. Dr. A. C. Bouquet says that 'he interpreted history dialectically, and saw it as the field of a long series of class-conflicts in which the familiar triad of thesis, antithesis and synthesis took the form of a collision between two opposing economic structures, leading to the emergence of a third and new economic order, which in its turn begat an opponent, and so on until, with the final arrival of the classless society, no further class-conflict was possible'. Reform and progress could come then, as Mervyn Stockwood puts it, only 'from the relentless class struggle which centres around the ownership of the means of production'.

The Communist Manifesto was not only concerned, however, with economic questions, but also with religion. Following the teaching of Ludwig Feuerbach in his *Essence of Christianity*, Marx rejected the idea of a God, and declared that religion was merely the opium of the people. The Manifesto plainly states that 'Communism abolishes eternal truths, it abolishes all religion and all morality'. 'Atheism,' wrote Lenin subsequently, 'is a natural and inseparable part of Marxism.' 'We will grapple with the Lord God in due season,' said Zinoviev in 1924. 'We shall vanquish Him in His highest heaven.' The official programme of the Soviet Party, published in 1932, states that one of the Party's objects is 'the real emancipation of the working masses from religious prejudices' and that, to this end, it 'organises the widest possible ... anti-religious propaganda'. Communism denies the existence of God and challenges Him in His highest heaven.

To achieve their end, Communists are prepared to act without scruple or shame, to lie, deceive and to sacrifice anything. The Communist ideology is perhaps most dangerous because it is an outright attack upon religion. John declared that one of the signs of the last times was the presence of antichrists (1 John 2:18): surely they are here already.

There are indications in the Bible that Russia has also a role to play on the prophetic stage. In Daniel 11:5–35 the prophet outlined with meticulous accuracy the story of the wars, intrigues and alliances of the Seleucids of Syria and the Ptolemies of Egypt down to the times of the Maccabees. Then, in verse 36, he introduced a king who was to suffer attacks from other powers located to the south and to the north of his own country (i.e. in the same direction as Egypt and Syria previously). Of this king there is no record in history, but it is evident that he must be a ruler in Israel. What Daniel portrayed, therefore, related to the future and implied that, at some subsequent date, Israel was to experience an invasion from Egypt, and a counter-invasion from some power in the north. That Egypt will again attack Israel cannot be doubted: the indignity of three defeats in two decades has only intensified Egyptian hatred of her neighbour, and the desire for revenge will inevitably provoke another assault. Russia has completely replaced the arms and equipment lost in the 1967 war and her naval vessels and strategic bombers have for some time been familiarising themselves with the Egyptian waters and Egyptian terrain, while Egypt is flooded with Russian technicians and advisers.

The assistance given has obviously not been for altruistic reasons. Although the U.S.S.R. seems to be encouraging a further onslaught upon Israel, there are potent reasons why she should not allow Egypt to seize control of the Middle East. Perhaps the most important is the tremendous oil deposits in the region. A few years ago, the American Institute of Mining, Metallurgical and Petroleum Engineering estimated that the Middle East has 68 per cent of the world reserves of oil. There are rich deposits in Bahrein, Iran, Iraq, Kuwait, Qatar and Saudi-Arabia, but the Sinai Peninsula has also vast untapped resources. Oil is a major sinew of war, and if Russia was contemplating an armed conflict with other powers, her most probable first step would be to move into the oil-producing countries and take control of them. She would certainly never tolerate their falling into the hands of Egypt. Nor would she suffer Egypt to cut her off from the warm-water ports of the south. Her re-equipment of Egypt is patently with the object of inspiring fresh trouble for Israel, but never to give Egypt possession of that country.

It is significant that Daniel predicts that, when Egypt attacks Israel at some future date, the northern forces will sweep through the country like a whirlwind, taking half the city of Jerusalem and leaving havoc and devastation in their train, driving the Egyptians back into their own country (Isa. 28:18, 19; Dan. 11:40-43; Joel 2:2-10, 20; Zech. 14:2). The complete destruction caused in Egypt is vividly told in Ezek. 30:1-8. The description of military and naval might given by Daniel makes it clear that the reference is not to some small nation like the Lebanon or Syria, but to a world power of great military might, and one is driven inescapably to the conclusion that the picture painted by the prophet is of the great anti-God nation of Russia. In view of current conditions, these events may, of course, be not very remote.

At the height of the northerner's triumph in Egypt, the Bible discloses that disturbing tidings will reach him from the north-east, in consequence of which he will immediately return in fury to devastate Israel (Dan. 11:44). The nature of the tidings is not revealed in Scripture, but there are two possible explanations. Since Israel will apparently be in alliance with a western power at that time (Dan. 9:27), the news may well be of an intervention from the west to deliver the captured city of Jerusalem. This is only a partial explanation, however, and the primary reference is undoubtedly to the descent of Christ to Mount Olivet to wage war against His people's foes, for the result is the complete destruction of the northern armies (Isa. 31:4-9, 59:18-20; Dan. 11:45). If the attack of Gog described in Ezekiel 39 has reference to the same army and the same period, verses 1-12 give some impression of the utter defeat suffered.

Russia is basically an anti-God nation. She has dared to shake her fist in the face of the Eternal and to declare contemptuously that no God exists. In His own time, the Almighty will crush this impudent and atheistic power. None may stand against Him and escape with impunity. But already what is foretold in Biblical prophecy seems to be casting its shadow before and the end seems almost in sight.

9

EGYPT AND HER FUTURE

IN *The Story of Mankind*, Henrik Willen Van Loon says that, primarily because of its fertility, 'the valley of the Nile had developed a high stage of civilisation thousands of years before the people of the west'. There were certainly prehistoric settlements at several centres, and some archaeologists have maintained that there are traces of human habitation dating as far back as 5,000 B.C. The annual inundation of the river deposited a layer of rich and fertile clay on both banks and converted the valley into one of the most fruitful areas on earth: so much so, in fact, that Egypt became known as the granary of the world. In consequence, settlers came from east and south to take advantage of the rich farm-lands available. Strabo indicates that ancient Egypt was relatively small in area, but was able to support a very large population.

The original inhabitants of the country were descendants of Mizraim, one of the sons of Ham (Gen. 10:6), and the country was first named Mizraim, although it was also referred to as Kemet, or the black land. Its present name was derived at a later date from the Greek Ægyptos. The ancient Egyptians were extremely industrious and seem to have engaged in various forms of manufacture as well as their principal occupation of agriculture. They were renowned for their learning and were the inventors of the art of writing (using hieroglyphics) as well as of a calendar which for long proved invaluable.

The early history of the country is lost in the mists of antiquity, but in 280 B.C. a priest named Manetho, who was keeper of the sacred archives, compiled a history, covering the period 3,200 B.C. to 332 B.C. According to Manetho these 29 centuries were spanned by 30 royal dynasties, but this is patently incorrect and there is no completely reliable record of the earlier periods of history. It is known that the land suffered repeated conquests and that the original Hamites were, on many occasions, brutally maltreated by Semitic and other invaders. In 1730 B.C. the country was attacked with horses and chariots by the Hyksos, or shepherd kings, from Arabia. One of these kings was the Pharaoh of Genesis 12 : 14–20, and it was during their régime that Joseph became prime minister of Egypt and that Jacob and his family removed to the land of Goshen (Gen. 46 : 29–34). The savage Hyksos rulers were thoroughly detested by the Egyptians. The Israelites, being shepherds themselves, found favour with Pharaoh, but shared the opposition attached to all shepherds by the inhabitants of the land. It was nearly two centuries before the Hyksos were driven out and a new dynasty founded. The following five centuries were one of the most glorious periods of Egyptian history : Asia as far east as the Euphrates came under the control of the new kingdom. The Israelite exodus took place soon after the expulsion of the Hyksos. From 1085 B.C. onwards Egypt's power and prestige began to decline, and the country fell successively into the hands of the Ethiopians, Persians and Macedonians and, although she was at times able to throw off the yoke of foreign conquerors, she never regained her former position of glory.

Ezekiel 32 gives some indication of the humiliation of Egypt's rulers as they were brought down with shame to the pit. Of this period J. H. Breasted has pertinently written in his *History of Egypt*, 'The fall of Egypt and the close of her characteristic history were already an irrevocable fact long before the relentless Cambyses knocked at the doors of Pelusium. The Saitic state was a creation of rulers who looked into the future, who belonged to it, and had little or no connection with the past. They were as essentially non-Egyptian as the Ptolemies who followed the Persians. The Persian conquest in 525 B.C., which deprived Psamtik III, the son of Amasis, of his throne and kingdom, was but a change of rulers, a purely external fact. And if a feeble burst of national feeling enabled this or that Egyptian to thrust off the Persian yoke for a brief period, the moment may be likened to the convulsive contractions which sometimes lend momentary motion to limbs, from which conscious life has long departed. With the fall of Psamtik III, Egypt belonged to a new world, toward the development of which she had contributed much, but in which she could no longer play an active part. Her great work was done, and unable, like Nineveh and Babylon, to disappear from the scene, she lived on her artificial life for a time under the Persians and the Ptolemies, ever sinking, till she became merely the granary of Rome, to be visited as a land of ancient marvels by wealthy Greeks and Romans.... But her unwarlike people, still making Egypt a garden of the world, show no signs of an awakening and the words of the Hebrew seer, "There shall be no more a prince out of the land of Egypt", have been literally fulfilled.' The Saracens from A.D. 641 and the Mamelukes and their successors for the seven centuries from A.D. 1250 were all foreign rulers, and the present ruler, President Nasser, is of Arabian and not Egyptian stock. Prophecy has certainly been fulfilled.

The Macedonians took the country in 332 B.C., but after the death of Alexander the Great, there was a certain amount of disorder until his vast empire was eventually divided between four of his generals. Ptolemy Soter took Egypt, Cyrene, Cyprus and Palestine and founded the dynasty of the Ptolemies, while Seleucus took the north and became the founder of the royal house of the Seleucidæ. These two powers, located to the south and the north of Palestine, played a considerable part in the history of that country and it fell a prey alternately to Egypt and Syria. Daniel 11 tells the story of the intrigues, alliances and wars of the two great powers down to the time of Antiochus Epiphanes, and then, leaping over the centuries, describes their future in a day still future (Dan. 11 : 36–45).

At the date of the New Testament, Egypt was a Roman province, having been captured by Augustus in 30 B.C. There was a large Jewish community in Alexandria and the gospel was brought to that city by John Mark, who suffered martydom there for his faith. The Coptic church owed its origin to Mark's evangelistic labours in Egypt. In the seventh century A.D., however, the Arabs swept over the country and a large percentage of the population turned from their own gods or from Christianity to embrace the faith of Islam. The Arabs settled in the country and although most of the *fellahin* today are probably descendants of the ancient Egyptians, many of the present inhabitants owe their origin to the Moslem invaders. It would hardly be correct, nevertheless, to describe Egypt as an Arab country.

The conditions in which the majority of the people lived steadily deteriorated, particularly during the Turkish régime. There was certainly a considerable improvement from 1882 onwards, during the British protectorate, but even today the mud villages crowding the restricted area of the Nile valley tell their own story. Once famous for its cotton and linen, glass and porcelain, Egypt formerly enjoyed a prosperity which its present impoverished inhabitants have never known. Moreover, the military activities of Gamal Abd an-Nasir (Nasser), who became prime minister in 1954, following the *coup d'etat* two years earlier, and then president in 1956, brought only further distress to the country.

Egypt's present bitter hostility to Israel is of no recent origin, although it has unquestionably received a strong impetus in the last few years, particularly since the formation of the United Arab Republic. The Arab hatred for the Jew dates back to the enmity between Ishmael and Isaac and between Esau and Jacob (Gen. 21 : 9; 27 : 41) and this has never diminished. Over the centuries it has grown, consistently and, as Ezekiel 35 : 5 predicted, it has become a permanent hatred. Although Egypt is not strictly an Arab country, President Nasser assumed the leadership of the Arab states and also absorbed the Arabic intense antagonism to the Jew. Egypt's own attitude may, in part, be an unconscious reflection of the events of centuries ago. The Egyptian's detestation of the Hyksos rulers extended to the Israelite shepherds of Goshen; as the descendants of Jacob multiplied numerically and increased in prosperity, fear was also mingled with hate. Lest the Israelites should become a serious threat to the country, they were subjected to a harsh servitude: their eventual exodus and the Divine destruction of the pursuing forces (Exod. 14 : 23–28) only added fuel to the fires of hatred. Egypt's inimical attitude was demonstrated on more than one occasion in history and Judah, in particular, suffered from her attacks (e.g. 1 Kings 14:26, 27).

In the last 20 years, Egyptian hatred for Israel seems to have reached its peak, and saboteurs and infiltrators have played their part in destroying peace. War has broken out three times, yet on each occasion the Arabs and Egyptians have been defeated. When the establishment of the Jewish state was proclaimed in 1948, 42 million Arabs surrounded half a million Jews and there seemed little doubt that the newly-formed State of Israel would be short-lived and that the Jews in Palestine would be driven into the sea. But the opposing forces were driven back and Israel was victorious. In 1956, Egypt, Syria and Jordan entered into a military alliance with one object—to exterminate the Jew. For a second time they failed in their purpose and Egypt and her allies were routed and the former suffered considerable loss. In 1967 President Nasser set out deliberately to provoke a war by the Arabs upon the Jews, determining this time to leave no Jew remaining in Palestine. Egypt was well-equipped with arms, tanks and military planes, and Israel was encircled by enemies: it only remained for the Arabs to close in. But amazingly, Israel was again victorious and Egypt lost most of her tanks, planes and equipment. There seems no doubt that the deliverance of Israel was a miracle. Three times in two decades God had intervened on behalf of His earthly people. Egypt which had inspired the war and had constantly breathed out threatenings, had suffered a humiliating defeat in the eyes of the world. She had been taught a lesson three times which could surely not be ignored.

But Egypt's attitude has not changed and she is now preparing for a fourth attack upon Israel. The arms and supplies lost during the brief 1967 war have been completely replaced by Russia, and Egypt is better equipped than ever before. There is little doubt that, before very long, a further attack will be made upon the hated state. There are clear indications in Daniel 11 that active opposition will again be demonstrated in the future. Apart from the desire for revenge for the humiliation and indignity inflicted upon Egypt by three defeats in two decades—and this by a relatively small nation far less well equipped and supplied—there is the constant irritation caused by the loss of revenues from the Suez Canal. When Egypt blocked the canal by sinking nine ships, she obviously did not foresee the consequences. Sand blown into the canal by the wind has reduced the depth of water to such an extent that 60 per cent of the shipping which previously used this route could no longer pass through the canal if it was re-opened. Even in normal circumstances, only ships of 60,000 tons could pass through the canal: but the oil companies are now ordering ships up to 312,000 tons and these would never be able to use the canal. It is true that Egypt is now discussing bypassing the canal by building a 207 mile oil pipeline from Suez to Alexandria at a cost of £50 million, but Israel is already constructing a similar pipeline from Eilat to Ashkelon at a cost of £40 million. Economics will presumably be the primary factor in deciding which pipeline is more successful, but the rivalry will provide an additional source of irritation.

Egypt has yet to reckon with God for her treatment of His people, and the prophetic Scriptures reveal that dark days lie before her in which Jehovah will mete out punishment, but there is also—astonishingly enough— a clear indication that ultimately, in the Divine purpose, she will be brought into blessing. In Isaiah 19 the prophet foretells Jehovah's coming in judgment to

Egypt, and pictures fear striking the hearts as civil war breaks out and city turns against city and district (*nome*) against district. The river will be stricken by God and the failure of the Nile will evidently result in economic disaster, administration will apparently break down, religion will fail and the complete loss of stability will create a state of panic among the people. At the same time, conditions will be worsened by the tyrannical despotism of the country's ruler. The prophet declares that Judah, so long the object of attack, will become a source of terror to Egypt. While the prophecy may have been partially fulfilled in the events of the past (not exluding those of 1967), its complete fulfilment obviously awaits a future day. In that day, according to Isaiah, the Egyptians will turn to God, Heliopolis and four other cities will go so far as to adopt the language of Canaan (this may be intended figuratively rather than literally, i.e. a pure manner of life) and swear allegiance to Jehovah, there will be a witness to God in the centre of the land (an altar) and on its border (a pillar), He will make Himself known to the Egyptians and, following His smiting of them, God will heal them. The chapter concludes with the complete reconciliation of Egypt, Israel and Assyria, a highway linking all three, and the Divine blessing being experienced by all three. (There are often fantastic interpretations of the 'altar' and the 'pillar' referred to by Isaiah, including a suggestion that the Great Pyramid is to play a part, but no satisfactory explanation has yet been furnished.)

In the same prophet's description of millennial conditions, he discloses that, at that date, God will recover His people a second time from Egypt and other countries, and that He will also dry up the Gulf of Suez and the Nile and its delta. But once again Isaiah refers to the highway from Assyria to Egypt (Isa. 11 : 11–16).

Again, in Ezekiel 29 and 30 the past and the future seem to be intertwined. The later prophet reveals further details of the judgment that is yet to fall upon the country. Egypt will then suffer for her treatment of Israel. She is to be destroyed by war and become completely desolate (see also Joel 3 : 19–21) and for 40 years utterly uninhabited, the people being scattered among the nations and dispersed into many countries. Nevertheless, they are to continue as a nation and are to be eventually restored to their own land, although in a state of humiliation. Obviously these predictions have never yet been fulfilled, but there are other indications in the prophetic word as to the time of their fulfilment.

After discussing the past relations of Syria and Egypt, Daniel 11 : 36–45 looks on to the future and reveals the events which are yet to occur at the end time. The future ruler of Israel at that date is described as an apostate Jew, who pays no regard to Jehovah or to the Messianic promise, and who is evidently a spiritist and under a diabolical control. 'At the time of the end,' Daniel declares, the king of the south (i.e. Egypt) will make an attack upon this ruler and his country—precisely as is expected today. When that invasion takes place, however, the prophet indicates that a northern power will sweep through Israel and the Middle East, devastating and plundering. But the primary object of this ferocious rampage will be the country of Egypt, and the prophecies already referred to give a vivid impression of the awful fate that will overtake that ancient land in the day of her trouble. Ezekiel declares that her foundations will be overthrown, the pride of her strength fall, her lands be desolated, and her cities laid waste (Ezek. 30 : 1–8). The proud land of the south will be relentlessly beaten down by the overwhelming strength and brutality of the invader, and all her treasures will fall into his hands. Moreover, when the sword falls upon Egypt, the northern army will evidently reach out to other countries, for anguish will seize Ethiopia and the men of Ethiopia and Libya will be slain by the sword (Ezek. 30:4, 5; Zeph. 2:12; Nah. 3:9). But at that critical moment, it appears that the Lord Jesus Christ will return to earth and utterly destroy the great northern hordes (Zech. 14:4; Dan. 11:45).

At the moment, Egypt may threaten God's people, but those who touch Israel touch the apple of God's eye, and Egypt will one day pay the price for what she has done over the centuries. Yet this was the country which afforded protection for God's Son (Matt. 2:13–15). Maybe this will be taken into account one day, but certainly—as already indicated—there seems to be a place of blessing for Egypt when our Lord sets up His earthly kingdom. Lands which have been hostile to each other will then be in perfect accord, and trade will pass freely from north to south and vice versa, and commercial prosperity obviously be enjoyed by all these countries.

It seems possible that the events predicted by Daniel will not long be postponed and that other prophecies concerning Egypt may, therefore, soon come to fulfilment. The picture is already shaping. But these events fall within a period after the end of the present Church era. If they seem to be imminent, how near must be the end of the age—and the return of our Lord Jesus Christ for His Church.

10

CHINA AND THE FAR EAST

THE early history of China may be dated so far back that it is almost lost in the mists of antiquity. As long ago as 3000 B.C. there were apparently human settlements in the valley of the Yellow River, and it is clear that the Chinese possessed their own culture and civilisation for centuries before the birth of Christ. Although, at the commencement of the present century, they were predominantly peasants rather than city dwellers, the level of Chinese civilisation was originally extremely high and the knowledge of the various sciences was very extensive. They may not perhaps have been the inventors of written language, but they certainly produced a highly sophisticated form of hieroglyphics in which 10,000 characters were in common use.

The country is one of the most populous in the world. At the beginning of the nineteenth century, its total population was already 400 million—that of the whole of Africa being only 250 million—and by the end of the twentieth century it is estimated that the figure will probably reach 4,000 million. The problem of providing sufficient food for such a large population grows daily more acute. Many of the poorer people in the past have enjoyed only one meal a day and have fed on leaves, tree bark, straw and grass, and cannibalism was not entirely unknown. The effect upon health and physique was disastrous. Prior to the present régime, according to one writer, 'millions of adults were ailing and dying, while tens of millions of children were growing up mis-shapen and diseased because they did not have enough to eat'. Although very few doctors exist the present rulers have checked the growth of disease and plagues such as cholera, smallpox, malaria and typhus. They have given repeated assurances that the people will not be allowed to starve, but these pledges are difficult to redeem. 'Food and land would be sought beyond the borders,' it is claimed, 'e.g. the rich lands of the north and the rice-producing areas in Cambodia, Vietnam, Burma and Thailand,' and even in distant but fertile areas of the African Continent. Involvement in military action in order to find means of satisfying the hunger of the people is not, therefore, a contingency which can be excluded, and it may provide the background to the military moves envisaged in the Book of Revelation.

China has never been deeply affected by the Christian faith. Her indigenous religion is Confucianism. Confucius was born in 550 B.C., when China was without a strong central government and the people were subject to marauding bandits who pillaged and murdered at will. The Chinese had a deepseated belief in and fear of devils and a great respect for their deceased ancestors, but Confucius was the first to introduce some form of philosophic religion—a change of heart by right living and right thinking. By the time of his death in 478 B.C. the majority of the kings and princes of China had accepted his teachings. His contemporary, Lao-Tse, founded another philosophic system known as Taoism, but his teachings were subsequently buried under a mass of superstition which completely vitiated their value. Disciples of Buddhism also began to move across the Himalayas and to propagate the wisdom of Siddhartha.

Christianity was not introduced into the country until A.D. 635, but it never really displaced Confucianism and always remained very largely a foreign religion in which relatively few Chinese were interested, and eventually it died out. For a thousand years, the message of the gospel was carried to the country spasmodically and almost incidentally by merchants and traders, who travelled to conduct their business, either overland to Sinkiang or by sea to the Chinese coast. The propagation of the gospel was not their primary concern and their testimony made little impact on the people. When, in A.D. 1600, Christian missionaries entered China, no native believers could be traced, and, accompanied as they were by traders, the heralds of the Cross did not adopt the most judicious course. When they came to a statue of Buddha or a picture of Confucius, to quote Van Loon, 'they came to the easy conclusion that these strange divinities were just plain devils, who represented something idolatrous and heretical. . . . Whenever the spirit of Buddha or Confucius seemed to interfere with the trade in spices and silks, the European attacked the "evil influences" with bullets and grapeshot,' leaving a heritage of ill-will.

For a long period the country was ruled by kings and princes of Chinese origin, concluding with the Ming dynasty. The latter eventually came to an end by their forcible supersession by foreign Manchu rulers. These controlled the country for at least two centuries. The 150 years up to the end of the nineteenth century proved, however, to be the period of China's greatest glory, although it is claimed today that the present Mao régime has eclipsed all its predecessors in the alleged prosperity enjoyed by the people and the extent of the geographical area they now occupy.

Up to the commencement of the nineteenth century,

only a few merchants were permitted to enter China; for all practical purposes it was hermetically sealed off and impenetrable by the west. 'The mounting pressure of the Occident did not make its first breaches in Chinese isolation until the 1840's,' says Prof. K. S. Latourette, 'and it was not until 1895 that the wall of Chinese resistance to westernisation crumbled. From that time on . . . the Occidental flood poured in. China was in revolution as it had never before been in all its long history. The Confucian monarchy fell, and the system of education based upon Confucianism was swept aside. Every phase of Chinese life was being altered.' The western 'invasion' was not entirely to the benefit of the nation, however. The western powers sought (and Russia and Japan seized) territorial and other concessions and did their utmost to exploit the country for their own advantage. Chinese sovereignty was restricted by treaties entered into or imposed in the last two centuries, and there was a general feeling of frustration and resentment, which became accentuated by the flowing tide of nationalism. As one writer remarks, 'Extraterritoriality, the fixing of tariffs by treaty, and the leaseholds, the concessions, and the settlements of foreign powers which dominated most of the chief ports were peculiarly irritating.'

This was the position at the outbreak of the First World War. The result was inevitable. For a quarter of a century or more, the country was convulsed by a revolution which affected every phase of life—political, religious, educational, social and economic—and which was further complicated by the external problems of war and invasion. The old faiths of Confucianism, Taoism and Buddhism were undermined and completely lost their appeal to the younger generation. Christianity, which had never secured a very great hold, strangely enough, seemed to gain a measure of strength and young converts demonstrated their willingness to pay the price for their loyalty to their faith.

A new party, the Kuomintang, was founded by Sun Yat-Sen, but unfortunately he died in 1925. A National Government was set up in Canton, and Chiang Kai Shek was appointed Commander-in-chief of the Nationalist Revolutionary Army. Chiang was not willing to remain indefinitely in a subordinate position, however, and in 1927 he seized the power and immediately commenced to modernise the country. His ruthlessness and the corruptness of his government caused most Chinese to execrate both, and ultimately the inevitable civil war broke out, and under the leadership of Mao Tse Tung, the people fought and put Chiang to flight. In 1949 the new Chinese People's Republic was proclaimed and Mao was appointed chairman. Chiang and his allies still hoped to dominate the country, but it was a forlorn hope, and he has now little prospect of recovering any part of the mainland. For the last 20 years Mao has been supreme and his own brand of Communism has been adopted.

Karl Marx interpreted history dialectically and he saw no prospect of any improvement in the condition of the proletariat short of a complete economic and political revolution (see chapter 8). Mao Tse Tung adopted this view unreservedly. In his *Selected Works*, he says, for example, 'the fact is that the great peasant masses have risen to fulfil their historic mission and that the forces of rural democracy have risen to overthrow the forces of rural feudalism. The patriarchal— feudal class of local tyrants, evil gentry and lawless landlords has formed the basis of autocratic government for thousands of years and is the corner-stone of imperialism, warlordism and corrupt officialdom. To overthrow these feudal forces is the real objective of the national revolution.' Millions of Chinese were marked out by the new régime for liquidation. In *Spotlight on Asia*, G. Wirt says that two million 'bandits' were liquidated by 1952. He explains that a 'bandit' means anybody who possesses a little land or who was regarded by the communists as dangerous to the régime. The opportunity has certainly been taken to dispose of many against whom those in authority had a grudge.

Communism is, of course, basically atheistic and aims at the abolition of religion. The government of the People's Republic has been responsible for an onslaught upon religion of all kinds, and many a Christian has paid with his life for his faith in Christ.

China today is sometimes said to be as isolationist as ever. 'She arrogantly proclaims her self-sufficiency,' says C. R. Hensman. 'She has thus expressed in contemporary terms her traditional notion of China as "the centre country". The Chinese have deliberately rejected attempts by outsiders to communicate with them and do not believe that they have anything useful to learn or receive from Europe and America. They have lost touch with reality. It was in the same way that the old Chinese Empire treated outsiders with scant deference and referred to them as barbarians. Chinese newspapers and broadcasts give the impression that the people of the whole world disagree with the attitude of their own governments and instead look up to China and Chairman Mao with admiration and gratitude. Because of this delusion, China has been less interested in having diplomatic relations with the major European powers and the United States than in establishing them with minor countries in the rest of the Third World.' On the other hand, as President Johnson pointed out in 1965, the Mao régime 'has destroyed freedom in Tibet, has attacked India, and has been condemned by the U.N. for aggression in Korea. It is a nation which is helping the forces of violence in almost every continent. The contest in Vietnam is part of a wider pattern of aggressive purposes.'

Thirty years ago Mao said that China's aim was a permanent peace throughout the world. 'In order to achieve this objective,' he said, 'we must wage a life and death war, must be prepared to sacrifice everything, and must fight to the last until our aim is achieved. The sacrifice may be great and the time long, but there already lies clearly before us a new world of permanent peace and permanent light.' China today is employing every possible subversive technique in quite a number of countries, and Robert MacNamara, then U.S. Defence Secretary, was justified in declaring that the Peking government had apparently embarked on a programme of global conquest that might eventually engulf the whole western world.

China's potential in this respect is not always realised. It has been stated that she already has 200 million men and women in the militia (including the home guard), who are under training for military operations, and that by 1970 the total will be 250 million. By 1975 she will be well equipped, not only with a large quantity of medium-range nuclear missiles, but also with intercontinental missiles of far more extensive range (possibly of 6,000 miles), and with a considerable number of rocket-firing submarines. She has at least four plants producing nuclear material—presumably for military purposes—and has now enough uranium 235 to produce 60 hydrogen bombs. It is anticipated that by 1975 she will have a stockpile of at least 100 such bombs. China has also shown an interest in the method of separating uranium 235 from uranium 238 by the ultra-centrifuge process instead of the expensive gaseous diffusion process at present employed and, in the foreseeable future, may be able to manufacture bombs at a relatively low cost.

The complete ruthlessness of the present régime indicates that nothing will be allowed to thwart the aims of the rulers. According to reports, far more people are dying in China than in the Vietnam war. Bodies periodically float down the Pearl River to Hong Kong. Mao has blocked the river with a flotilla of small sampans and fishing boats to prevent bodies reaching Hong Kong, and 8,000 bodies are known to have been fished out by this 'sampan navy'. Reports leak out of murder and atrocity on an unparalleled scale and it is clear that the control of the country is absolute. Mao Tse Tung is constantly glorified and R. S. Elegant says in *The Centre of the World*, 'Never previously has a single individual been so exalted, for never previously have the mythmakers controlled so efficiently an apparatus of publicity directed at such an enormous captive audience. . . . He has repeatedly demonstrated that he will kill to impose his version of truth—or to evoke the adulation which is essential to his assumption of omniscience. Truth, for Mao Tse Tung, is what he makes it.' When the tremendous power held in the hands of a few (and ultimately in the hands of one man) is realised, the awful potentialities may more easily be envisaged. As one writer points out, 'her immense labour communes (of which there are 7,000), her growing industrial potential, her belligerent communism, her terrifying growth rate and population, the critical food situation, and her keen interest in Africa' disturb the mind of the thinking man.

The last two points are of particular significance.

Food is rationed and prices controlled. Many people have more to eat than they formerly had, but many still suffer from malnutrition. The exploding population is accentuating the need to discover fresh supplies of food. The same writer points to 'Africa, huge, relatively fertile, politically divided, poorly armed and unorganised', and sees a relevance in the great highway which is being constructed by China to the north of India, but he emphasises that the only land bridge to Africa is Palestine. Is there really any significance in this? It is true that there are a score of Chinese diplomatic missions established in Africa and that she is patently engaged in subversive activities in that continent, but the long journey required for an invasion of Africa seems to make this a fantastic impossibility. China has offered to build the essential Zambia–Tanzania railway, to the Zambian copper belt, in five years at the cost of £115 million. This is only a precursor to the events of the end time.

It is interesting to note that the prophet Isaiah refers to the regathering of Israel in a future day from various quarters, including 'the east' and 'the land of Sinim' (Isa. 43:5; 49:12). The wilderness of Sin and Mount Sinai lie, of course, to the south of Palestine and are obviously not sufficiently remote to satisfy the implications of the prophecy. The classical Sinæ referred to China and it seems fairly evident that Isaiah's reference was also to that country. J. D. Davis states that 'the presence of Israelites in China is attested as early as the third century B.C. and it is not known how much earlier they migrated to that land'. When Jehovah regathers His ancient people and restores them to their own land, therefore, the Orient will be among the areas from which they will be drawn.

There are other Biblical references, however, which

are of even greater interest in some respects. After the sounding of the sixth Apocalyptic trumpet, the angel was Divinely directed to release the four spirits who were 'bound in the great river Euphrates', and these gathered a terrifying army of 200 million to destroy a third of mankind (Rev. 9:13–19). When the vials of Divine wrath were subsequently poured out, 'the sixth angel poured out his vial upon the great river Euphrates; and the water thereof was dried up, that the way of the kings of the east might be prepared'. The mighty armies from the 'sunrising' (as the word 'east' should really be rendered) were then gathered, together with the armies of the other great world-powers, to 'a place called in the Hebrew tongue Armageddon' (Rev. 16:12–16). Some writers have laid stress in recent days on the 200 million army of Revelation 9:16 and the size of the present Chinese militia, but it is probably unwise to draw comparisons of this kind, although it is difficult to avoid the conclusion that the great leaders from the sunrising cannot refer to any but the great land of China.

It is interesting to note that, according to *The Jerusalem Post*, the Chief of the Chinese Army General Staff has pledged the support of China in the armed struggle of the Arab nations against Israel. He declared that the Chinese army was stronger than ever and denounced the U.S. and Soviet attempts to reach a solution to the Middle East problem as purely political. It is clear that China intends to take a part in the solution of the problem—and that the part she plays will not be for Israel's benefit. But this is just what the Word of God discloses.

Under the terms of the Abrahamic covenant, the 1,700-mile-long Euphrates is to be the eastern boundary of the land of Israel in a future day (Gen. 15:18). It was the diversion of the river Euphrates from its normal course through the centre of Babylon, leaving the river bed dry, that allowed Darius to capture the city on the night of Belshazzar's feast (Dan. 5:31). The Euphrates, as Prof. J. F. Walvoord points out in *The Nations In Prophecy*, 'forms the eastern boundary of the ancient Roman Empire, as well as the prophesied eastern boundary of the land which God promised to the seed of Abraham (Gen. 15:18; Deut. 1:7; 11:24; Josh. 1:4). In Isa. 11:15 and Zech. 10:11, there is a similar prediction of the drying up of the Euphrates River, although the name of the river is not mentioned.' Whether or not the implication of the Apocalyptic passages is that the river will actually be dried up, it is clearly implied that any barrier to an invasion from the Orient will be removed, and that a tremendous army will move towards the land of Israel for the final world conflict in the Middle East.

The picture painted by the prophetic Word may not be so remote as it might at first sight seem. There can be no dubiety about China's intentions. If the doctrines of Communism have been diluted in Russia, they still remain undiluted in China, and that country, having shaken off the shackles of years of western bondage, seems now determined to implement the basic principles of Communism and to involve the world in a struggle of life and death. Any military movement would eventually be of necessity to the west. If, in addition, there is any substance in the theory that Chinese interest in the African continent is based upon her need for food and for land in which to grow food, there would be further reason for moving westward. The distance to be traversed is tremendous and naturally creates doubt as to the interpretation of the Biblical prophecies, but a more careful examination of current trends and of the Scriptural statements themselves seems to leave little room for doubt.

Zechariah 14:2, 3 declares that all nations will be gathered to the Middle East and that Jerusalem will be sacked, its women raped and half of its population carried away captive. But, in the day of Israel's extremity, the Lord will come forth to deliver His people and to destroy their foes. Many of the predictions of the Scriptures seem today to be nearing fulfilment, and those which relate to the 'yellow peril' of the Orient are now beginning to appear more logical than ever before. How imminent then may be the event which is to precede them, viz. the return of Christ for His church (1 Thess. 4:15–17).

11

SIGNS OF THE TIMES

In the preceding chapters, reference has been made to current trends and occurrences as an indication that the events of which Biblical prophecy speaks cannot be very remote from the present day. Indeed some of the developments and happenings of today seem undoubtedly to presage those events. That history is fast hastening to some climax can scarcely be questioned. The existing order is in danger of disruption by tendencies working from within as well as by forces assailing from without.

'A civilisation reaches a certain point,' wrote Christabel Pankhurst in *Pressing Problems of the Closing Age*, 'decays from within, is attacked from without, and finally dies. Another civilisation then rises to its height and, like its predecessors, dies. History is the record of this process often repeated. What does it mean? The question is vital, is urgent for us today, because the world crisis is rapidly developing and will affect each individual life and every nation even more directly and far more seriously than did the last war. For our guidance, from day to day, we must have, here and now, a true science, a true philosophy of history. The Bible alone gives us this. It shows us a world at variance with God, and world-civilisation decaying and dying in consequence.' We seem to be reaching the end. Something must inevitably happen—and soon. But what? The Christian answers unhesitatingly that everything that is occurring today is indicative of the imminence, not merely of some event, but of the personal return of the Lord Jesus Christ for His people. That event cannot long be delayed.

To quote Christabel Pankhurst again (and we make no apology for quoting *in extenso*)—this time from her book *The World's Unrest*, 'A striking parallel can be drawn between the world as it is now, at the approach of the Second Advent, and the world as it was at the approach of the First Advent. Then, as now, the times were distressful. Then, as now, wars and rumours of wars produced exhaustion and engendered fears. Then, as now, democratic institutions, as understood at that period, were in practice breaking down, unable to cope with the extraordinary conditions of the time. Then, as now, many were looking for some strong man, some superman, in whose hands they and all their concerns should be safe. Then, as now, the Roman Empire was coming, and finally did come, into being. Then, as now, the misery and despair of some was discordantly accompanied by the hilarity and riotous living of others.

'Then, as now, the realisation of human defencelessness against dangers existing in the visible and invisible realms was moving many to yearn for divine protection, and the consciousness of human sin was moving them to yearn for divine redemption. Then, as now, the religious sense of many was confused, perplexed by a multiplicity of creeds and cults competing for their adherence. Then, as now, there was, on the part of some at least, the longing for a present, a visible God—for "God manifest in the flesh". Then, as now, there were Jews . . . looking for the advent of Messiah. They believed the world's trials, present and prospective, to be the "pangs of Messiah", the signs that heralded the promised coming of Messiah. Then, that expectation of Messiah's coming was about to be literally and really fulfilled, so far as His predicted advent to suffer humiliation and death was concerned. Now, with the same literalness and reality, the expectation of Messiah's coming is about to be again fulfilled—this time, as regards His predicted advent with power and in great glory.'

We believe that the end times may very well be in sight and that the events which are to happen after the Lord's return for His church are, in all probability, being foreshadowed in the circumstances and conditions of the present day. If that be so, then the departure of the Christian must be close at hand, and the Master's promise to come again for His own may soon be redeemed. 'For the Lord Himself will descend from heaven with a shout, with the voice of the archangel and with the sound of the trumpet of God. And the dead in Christ will rise first: then we who are alive, who are left, shall be caught up together with them in the clouds to meet the Lord in the air; and so shall we always be with the Lord' (1 Thess. 4 : 16, 17).